What can I bring?

Sophie Hansen

What can I bring?

Easy, delicious food for sharing

murdoch books

Sydney | London

Spring.

Summer.

Autumn.

Winter.

'What can I bring?'

This is how I respond when invited to a gathering. It's how many of us do, I think.

We all want to contribute, be helpful, and bring something to the table. But what? I have a wall of cookbooks and a phone full of saved recipes, but when the reply pings back, 'a salad would be great' or 'maybe something sweet', my mind goes blank. It's a bit to do with too much choice, a bit to do with wanting to bring something really good and different, and a bit to do with general decision overwhelm.

So, what should we bring? We want to do ourselves (and said cookbook collections) proud, and bring something that people will be excited to eat and that is easy to transport, bring together at the last minute and share with those we love.

It's a tough brief. Or, rather, was a tough brief, because I've just spent a year working it out for all of us, and the answers are here in this book. *What Can I Bring?* is an instant, easy and delicious guide to what to bring for and to any occasion.

From wintry picnics to progressive dinner parties, fundraising cake stalls, birthday dinners (you're on cake, no pressure) and the annual camping trip, this book has us covered. And because the idea is 'portable food, but make it special', every recipe is forgiving, generous and (mostly) happy to sit out at room temperature for a while. In other words, the best kind.

It's not just a collection of ideas for what to bring when invited somewhere, it's also a celebration of honest, country-style hospitality. Because while I know that this spirit of generosity runs deep everywhere, I live in the country, and it's been my experience that the 'bring a plate' culture grows stronger the further inland you go.

Maybe it's because we all travel that bit further for gatherings, or because they're often that bit bigger in scale (paddock parties for one hundred are common). Either way, droughts, floods or budgets don't stop us coming together at shared tables. We always bring something. And our gatherings are easier, and more affordable, inclusive and interesting for it.

In every community, I've found that the instinctive reaction to any collective or individual event – be that a tragedy, celebration or natural disaster – is coming together to make and share food. This is especially so when life feels out of control; we can always gather, contribute a plate and enjoy the simple pleasure of eating good food. It might seem like a small thing on paper but it's big, real and joyful in practice.

Also, when everyone contributes something, it not only puts less pressure on the host, but it makes things way more interesting. Don't you love seeing what people bring to parties? It's a fascinating look into who they are and how they like to celebrate. It's about getting to know that friend a little better because you heard the story behind the cake, or learning the memories that are tied up in the jar of special barbecue sauce.

There is such a rich diversity of cultures and flavours across country Australia; here is just a taste from my small corner of it. While most of the recipes in this book are mine, some have come from friends who agreed to contribute their recipes for the dishes that they love and share most. Generosity is at the heart of cooking and I hope this book celebrates this in the most delicious way possible.

I hope you enjoy cooking from and reading this book, and see it as the open and generous invitation I want it to be: to gather, share and feed the people you love with dishes that mean the world.

How to transport food, host and be hosted

GENERAL FOOD SAFETY ADVICE
This is general information only; check online for more detailed information on storing and transporting food safely.

- Store cold food at 4°C (39°F) and below; keep hot food above 140°C (275°F). If in doubt, invest in a basic thermometer (they're not expensive) and occasionally check your food en route.
- If transporting food hot, make sure it's piping hot when you leave the house. The same goes with cold; food should be thoroughly chilled.
- For serving at room temperature, as a general rule, food shouldn't be left out for longer than 2 hours.
- Make sure food stays covered to keep heat or cold in and flies out.

KEEPING FOOD HOT
- Insulated containers are great, but if you don't have any, go for the thickest-walled dishes you have (Dutch ovens are good too, though heavy). Wrap them in a couple of towels, then transport in a laundry basket or regular basket (if they fit!).
- Heat packs or even a hot water bottle make a big difference. Pack these at the bottom of an insulated cooler, place some newspaper on top, then the dish, then fill the space in the cooler with your picnic blanket or towels.
- Wrapped in a towel, your slow-cooker dish will keep things hot for ages, too.
- To keep pastry hot but not soggy, wrap a heat pack in paper towel and place it in the bottom of a casserole (or other thick-walled) dish. Place your pastry items on top – not wrapped in foil. And then wrap the dish lightly with a tea towel, allowing for some steam to escape. We want to avoid condensation here because that equals soggy pastry!
- If you have a wide-mouthed thermos, warm it up, then dry it completely and line the bottom with a few folded paper towels. Stack your hot sausage rolls (see page 28), Sambousek (page 172) or Ragu rolls (page 17) on top and pop the lid on.

KEEPING FOOD COLD
- The usual suspects are your friends here: an insulated cooler and lots of ice and ice packs.
- Fill your thermos with a handful of ice cubes to keep drinks ice cold.
- Find a tray or container that's just bigger than the one you'll fill with your salad or meat dish. Fill that with 3 cm (1¼ inches) water and freeze overnight until solid. Place under your food container, wrap in a tea towel and transport in an insulated cooler. (This works well for short periods, but the ice will eventually melt and spill if left too long.)
- Use smaller bowls and replenish them from the cooler or fridge as needed.

GENERAL TRANSPORT ADVICE
- With cakes and tarts, it's all about the base! Place on the flattest, biggest plate you have, then find a container, tin or box to fit it in. Line the container with a tea towel for stability and pack in neatly.
- Travel first, assemble later, especially with anything involving dairy and soft herbs. Or anything that could go soggy.
- We all know the best parties happen in the kitchen, so don't worry if your contribution needs to be assembled on arrival; just find a flat surface, grab a drink and join in!

HOSTING A 'BRING A PLATE' GATHERING

- Rule number one: never feel weird about asking your friends to contribute.
- But don't stretch the friendship! I usually take care of the main meal then invite friends to bring a salad, slice or some biscuits for dessert.
- Let your guests know what you're making so they can bring things to complement it. If you're preparing a big main course, like the shanks on page 164 or the tagine on page 217, let everyone know so they can match their sides and salads.
- Make it fun! Suggest a theme, a decade, a vibe, a style of cuisine – anything. That way, everyone will have a starting point when deciding what to bring.
- Don't forget the finer details: how many people are coming, whether you'll be near the house or on a picnic, and any dietary requirements.
- As a general rule, I'm allergic to spreadsheets, but if you're hosting a big event, a live document that everyone can add their contribution to can be helpful. Set it up, add your info and share to avoid double- or quadruple-ups. Then send the link to anyone who asks, 'What can I bring?'
- All of the above said, not everyone will have the time, headspace or inclination to cook something. That's cool. If they offer to contribute, maybe suggest some nice bread or similar? And only if they offer.

ATTENDING A 'BRING A PLATE' GATHERING

- As the title of this book suggests, 'What can I bring?' is a pretty standard reply to most invitations. But if your host says, 'Nothing, we're all sorted', then please take them at their word and let them plan the menu. Instead, bring a little gift to say 'thanks for having us'. There are loads of ideas on page 109.
- Bring whatever serving utensils/dishes you'll need for your dish.
- Don't assume there'll be fridge space; it's probably already heaving. Bring your drinks/dish/elements in an insulated cooler with plenty of ice, and don't even open that fridge door.
- Likewise, don't plan on getting much bench space. That will be at a premium, too. So, try to have everything chopped and ready to assemble on the lid of your cooler, or the tray of your car boot, or really any flat surface that's free!
- Be super aware of good food-safety practices. See opposite for some general guidelines, or hop online for some more information.
- Even if it's a huge gathering, your dish doesn't need to feed everyone. I generally make enough for six people.

Spring.

It's time to crack out the picnic basket! Winter's done and we're out of hibernation, so let's celebrate spring with catch-ups in the park, a big feast in the back garden, and long tables of salads, sides, cakes and slices to feed a crowd.

Feast.

Things to eat with one hand

Filling, substantial meals you can eat with one hand are handy in general, but they are especially useful for new parents who are cradling their little person, farmers at harvest time who are behind the wheel of a tractor, or party guests who have a drink in one hand. Or even for hosts who want to entertain a big crew but don't have enough seats. Here are some ideas to thrust into the free hands of all of the above.

Spring

Corn fritter and salmon 'sliders'

These sliders are great for feeding a big group. Make the fritters in advance, then just warm them and assemble the rolls when ready. Thanks to Tina Skipper, a wonderful country cook and gardener from northern New South Wales, for this inspiration. You can use chewy baguettes, as I do here, or swap in soft floury damper rolls, or even rich brioche rolls. The fritters and the dill sauce are also great as a salad - aka without the bread - it's just a bit more difficult to eat with one hand!

Prep time 20 mins
Cook time 15 mins
Serves 6–8

12–14 lettuce leaves
2 long baguettes, sliced into
  15 cm (6 inch) pieces, or bread
  rolls, to serve
450 g (1 lb) hot-smoked salmon

Fritters
4 cups (600 g) corn kernels (from
  about 4 cobs)
2 spring onions (scallions), white
  part only
3 eggs
1 bunch dill, finely chopped
1 tsp sea salt and freshly ground
  black pepper, to taste
1½ cups (225 g) self-raising flour
¼ cup (60 ml) olive oil, for frying

Dill mayonnaise
Remaining dill from the fritters
  (see method)
2 Tbsp capers, finely chopped
1 tsp dijon mustard
⅓ cup (85 g) mayonnaise
Lemon juice (optional)

Preheat the oven to 140°C (275°F).

To make the fritters, combine half the corn kernels, the spring onion, eggs, a small handful of the dill, the salt, pepper and flour in a food processor or blender and blitz until you have a lumpy mixture. Stir in the remaining corn kernels.

Heat a little olive oil in a large frying pan over medium–high heat and drop in about ⅓ cup (70 g) of the fritter mixture for each fritter. Use your spoon to spread the mixture into fritter shapes and cook for 1–2 minutes on each side or until golden and cooked through. Repeat with the remaining batter. Transfer the cooked fritters to a baking tray, cover with foil and keep warm in the oven until needed, or refrigerate and reheat before serving.

For the dill mayonnaise, mix all the ingredients together in a bowl and adjust the seasoning as needed.

When you're ready to assemble, place one or two pieces of lettuce on the bottom pieces of baguette, top with a fritter, a generous amount of the dill mayonnaise and some of the salmon, then secure the baguette 'lids' with a piece of twine, or wrap in a serviette.

Travel advice
These should hold up pretty well en route. But if you're going any distance, perhaps pack the elements separately in an insulated ice box or cooler and assemble on arrival.

Citrus juice ice cubes
Another wonderful idea from my friend Tina. This is such a refreshing drink to have on hand.

1. Squeeze some lemon, lime or orange juice (or a mixture) into ice-cube trays and freeze.
2. When packing up lunch for a hot day out, simply place some frozen juice cubes into a large insulated cooler of water.

Ragu rolls

This recipe is capital G Good: tender beef ragu baked into a soft roll with pickles and mozzarella. They are wonderful to make in a big batch and take anywhere people might want a filling, easy-to-eat roll of goodness. And, if you prefer, just cut out a step and fill some floury soft damper rolls with the ragu, sloppy-joe style. It's best to make the ragu the day before and let it cool down in the fridge before filling the rolls. That extra step helps with the assembly and makes for a better, more tender ragu.

Prep time 40 mins
Cook time 3 hours, plus proving
Makes 12

200 g (7 oz) mozzarella, thinly sliced
400 g (14 oz) dill pickles, drained and cut into 5 mm (¼ inch) slices
2 eggs, beaten, for the egg wash
¼ cup (40 g) sesame seeds

Ragu filling
1.2 kg (2 lb 12 oz) chuck steak, cut into 3–4 pieces
¼ cup (60 ml) olive oil
1 brown onion, finely chopped
1 carrot, finely chopped
2 celery stalks, finely chopped
¼ cup (60 g) tomato paste (concentrated purée)
1 tsp brown sugar
400 g (14 oz) tin whole peeled Italian tomatoes

Rolls
14 g (½ oz) dry yeast
30 g (1 oz) sugar
1 kg (2 lb 4 oz) 00 flour
1 tsp sea salt, plus extra for sprinkling
100 g (3½ oz) butter, cubed and softened

For the ragu, preheat the oven to 140°C (275°F). Season the beef well with salt and pepper. Heat half of the oil in a large ovenproof frying pan over medium heat and brown the meat well on all sides. Set aside.

Reduce the heat to low and add the remaining oil, onion, carrot and celery. Cook for 20 minutes, stirring often, until the vegetables have softened and are beginning to caramelise. Add the tomato paste, brown sugar and tinned tomatoes. Half-fill the tomato tin with water, swirl it around, and add that, too. Stir well and bring to a simmer.

Return the beef to the pan, cover and place in the oven for 2 hours, or until the beef is completely tender. Remove, then carefully transfer the ragu to a heatproof container and refrigerate to cool completely.

For the rolls, combine the yeast, sugar and 2 cups (500 ml) lukewarm water in the bowl of a stand mixer fitted with the dough hook attachment, or in a large mixing bowl. Whisk to combine and leave for a few minutes, or until the yeast begins to bubble. Add the flour, salt and butter and knead for 5 minutes, or until the dough is smooth and elastic and the butter its completely incorporated. Cover with a tea towel and leave in a warm place for 1 hour, or until doubled in size.

Line two baking trays with baking paper. Turn the dough out onto a benchtop and divide into 12 balls (about the size of a golf ball). Press a deep indentation into the middle of a ball and work it into a 'bowl' with sides about 1–2 cm (½–¾ inches) thick. Spoon 1–2 tablespoons of the ragu into the middle of the dough 'bowl', top with two slices of mozzarella and pickle, then bring the edges of the dough together to create a ball. Pinch the dough to create a seal and place, seam side down, on the lined tray. Repeat with the remaining dough, ragu, cheese and pickle. Leave to prove for another 30 minutes.

Preheat the oven to 200°C (400°F). Brush each roll with the egg wash. Sprinkle with sesame seeds and a little sea salt and bake for 25–30 minutes, or until the rolls are golden brown.

Travel advice
Bake the rolls just before heading off. Keep them warm by wrapping them in a couple of tea towels.

Aloo gobi wraps with spinach and crispy chickpeas

Aloo gobi is the first thing I order at our local Indian restaurant here in Orange, New South Wales. I love the comfort and softness of the potato lifted by the warm, bright spices. There are countless recipes for this popular dish; this is the one I love and make most at home. It's fabulous not only in these wraps but also on its own, perhaps with some brown rice, or with a fried egg on top. Similarly, the spinach sauce and chickpeas have many lives outside this recipe. The sauce is great on rice bowls, atop a curry, or spread over roti, and the chickpeas are great for a snack or tossed into a salad.

Prep time 40 mins
Cook time 1 hour 30 mins
Serves 4–6

Aloo gobi
2 Tbsp vegetable oil or ghee
1 brown onion, diced
2 garlic cloves, finely chopped
3 cm (1¼ inch) piece ginger, peeled and finely chopped (about 2 Tbsp)
1 tsp cumin seeds
½ tsp ground turmeric
½ tsp garam masala
½ tsp ground coriander
1 tsp sea salt
400 g (14 oz) potatoes, peeled and cut into 3 cm (1¼ inch) cubes
2 cups (250 g) cauliflower florets (about 1 small cauliflower)
400 g (14 oz) tin whole peeled Italian tomatoes
Juice of 1 lemon, or to taste
1 handful coriander (cilantro), roughly chopped

Spinach sauce
1 bunch spinach, or 300 g (10½ oz) defrosted frozen spinach
2 Tbsp olive oil
1 small brown onion, chopped
1 garlic clove, finely chopped
1 Tbsp finely chopped ginger

1 tsp ground cumin
½ tsp ground coriander
1 tsp sea salt
½ cup (130 g) Greek-style yoghurt
1 tsp brown sugar

Chickpeas
400 g (14 oz) tin chickpeas, drained and rinsed
2 Tbsp olive oil
1 tsp ground cumin
1 tsp ground turmeric
1 tsp chilli flakes

To assemble
Roti or chapati wraps (you can get these from the freezer section of many supermarkets, otherwise use plain white or wholemeal wraps)
Pickled red onions

What Can I Bring?

For the aloo gobi, heat the oil in a large saucepan over medium heat. Add the onion and cook for about 10 minutes, or until soft and translucent. Add the garlic, ginger, spices and salt and stir together. Cook for a couple of minutes, then add the potato and cauliflower, stir to combine, and cook for 5 minutes.

Pour in the tinned tomatoes then half-fill the tin with water, swirl it around, and add that, too. Reduce the heat, cover and cook until the potatoes and cauliflower are tender, about 45 minutes. Top up with more water as it cooks if needed.

Meanwhile, make the spinach sauce. If you're using fresh spinach, wash and shred the leaves from their stems. Place the still-wet leaves in a large frying pan or wok over medium heat and cook, tossing often, until the spinach is bright green and soft, about 3–5 minutes.

Set the spinach aside, wipe out the pan and add the oil. Now add the onion and cook for 5 minutes, or until soft. Add the garlic, ginger, spices and salt and cook for a few more minutes. Return the spinach to the pan. (If you're using frozen spinach, add it now.)

Transfer the mixture to a food processor or blender and leave to cool for 10 minutes. Add the yoghurt and sugar and blitz until you have a smooth, bright-green sauce. Check the flavour and adjust the seasoning to taste, then transfer to a jar and refrigerate till needed.

To make the chickpeas, preheat the oven to 200°C (400°F). Tip the chickpeas into a small roasting tin. Toss with the olive oil, spices and some salt and pepper and roast in the oven for about 20 minutes, tossing halfway through, until the chickpeas are crispy and golden. Leave to cool.

To assemble, sprinkle the lemon juice and coriander over the aloo gobi (you can serve it warm or at room temperature). Heat your wraps according to the packet instructions. Spread about 2 tablespoons of the spinach sauce in the middle of each wrap and place a little aloo gobi just off-centre. Top with the chickpeas and pickled red onion and wrap as tightly as you can. Repeat with the remaining wraps and fillings.

Travel advice

Depending on what you used to wrap these beauties, you might need to be quite gentle with them (I find the roti wraps – my favourite – tend to break quite easily). Keep cool until ready to share.

Indispensable savoury tarts

Of course, this book needed a good tart recipe or three. A base that can be tweaked over time and take (almost) any variation you can throw at it. A good savoury tart really is a no-brainer when it comes to taking something to a friend's party, gathering – anywhere. It can be cut into small pieces to share around, or bigger slices and served with salad for a whole meal.

This is the recipe I reach for most often when wanting to make something savoury with pastry. It's pretty forgiving, easy to handle and, importantly, really tasty. Likewise, the ricotta filling is a blank canvas that can take any cheese/vegetable/herb combination you fancy. Here are my favourites.

Above: Caramelised onion, cherry tomato, garlic and cheddar tart (page 22); Below right: Slab galette with greens, peas and 'almost everything' bagel seasoning (page 23)

Shortcrust pastry

Makes approx. 380 g (13½ oz) pastry,
or enough for 1 large tart or 8 small tarts

1⅔ cups (250 g) plain (all-purpose) flour,
   plus extra for dusting
A pinch of salt
½ cup (125 g) chilled butter, cubed
4 Tbsp iced water

Tip the flour onto your benchtop, add the salt and
make a well in the centre. Into this, place the chilled
butter. Using the heel of your hand, smoosh the butter
into the flour, working it together until the mixture is
coarse and sandy with pea-sized pieces of butter.
Now add the water, a little at a time, still using the
heel of your hand to bring everything together into
a cohesive disc of pastry. A few streaks and seams
of butter are totally fine here. Wrap in plastic wrap
and chill in the fridge for 30 minutes.

   Depending on your tin/tray size and depth, you
might have some left-over pastry. Just roll it out and
make yourself a mini tart.

Ricotta filling

This might make a bit too much filling, depending
on how many vegetables you're adding, or the size
of your tins/tarts, but if you do have a little extra,
let's say 1 cup (230 g), perhaps go for a quick baked
ricotta-ish situation. Simply add one or two more
eggs to the mixture, pour into a buttered ovenproof
dish and sprinkle with a little more cheese, then
bake at 180°C (350°F) till puffed and golden. Serve
with a simple green salad.

Makes approx. 400 g (14 oz)

2 eggs
½ cup (50 g) finely grated parmesan
½ cup (125 ml) single (pure) cream
⅔ cup (165 g) fresh, soft ricotta

Whisk all the ingredients together until well combined.

Caramelised onion, cherry tomato, garlic and cheddar tart

This tart, whether you make it as one big one or little baby ones, is an almost guaranteed crowd pleaser. You could leave out the onion if you think your crew would prefer it, but either way, I know that if you make and take this to your next street party (or similar), you'll definitely have smashed the brief.

<u>**Prep time**</u> 30 mins, plus chilling
<u>**Cook time**</u> 1 hour 35 mins
<u>**Serves**</u> 6–8

80 g (2¾ oz) butter
2 onions, thinly sliced
2 garlic cloves, thinly sliced
500 g (1 lb 2 oz) whole cherry
   tomatoes
2 Tbsp lemon or regular thyme
   leaves
1 tsp sea salt
½ tsp chilli flakes (optional)
1 × quantity Shortcrust pastry
   (page 21), chilled
Plain (all-purpose) flour,
   for dusting
1 × quantity Ricotta filling
   (page 21) made with 1 cup
   (100 g) grated cheddar
   instead of parmesan
grated parmesan, to serve

Melt half the butter in a heavy-based frying pan over medium heat and add the onion. Reduce the heat to low and cook gently, stirring every now and then, for about 30 minutes, or until the onion is completely soft and has turned a caramelised, deep-brown colour. Remove from the pan and set aside.

Return the pan to the heat and add the remaining butter and the garlic. Cook for 1 minute, then add the cherry tomatoes, thyme, salt and chilli flakes, if using. Lower the heat, cover and cook for about 5 minutes, or until the tomatoes burst but don't collapse. Remove the lid and transfer the tomato mixture to the bowl with the onions.

Roll the chilled pastry out onto a lightly floured benchtop until it is about 3 mm (⅛ inch) thick. Gently drape over your rolling pin and lower into a 24 cm (9½ inch) loose-bottomed tart tin (or a number of small tins, or whatever you have on hand). Press the pastry into the edges of your tin and trim any overhang. Place in the fridge for 30 minutes to chill.

Preheat the oven to 180°C (350°F).

Prick the base of the pastry a few times with a fork. Line with baking paper and fill with baking weights, rice, beans or similar. Blind bake for 10 minutes, then gently remove the paper and weights and return to the oven for another 10 minutes, or until the pastry looks and feels quite dry and is just turning the palest gold.

Using your fingers, pull out the tomato and onion from the mixture, leaving the juices behind. (Reserve any left-over liquid and whisk it with a little olive oil and balsamic for a quick dressing.) Scatter the onion and tomato on the base of your blind-baked tart shell.

Pour in the ricotta mixture and bake the tart for 35–40 minutes, or until puffed and golden. Serve topped with grated parmesan.

<u>Travel advice</u>
This is delicious at room temperature. If you're making it in the morning, just let it cool and then transport it in a container wrapped in a tea towel (don't put the lid on because you don't want condensation here, which leads to soggy pastry).

• *Pictured page 20*

What Can I Bring?

Slab galette with greens, peas and 'almost everything' bagel seasoning

Big, bright and green, this is a fresh take on our base tart recipe. Also, you don't need a tin or to bother with blind baking so it's pretty simple to put together. Make into small tarts or do one big one, cut into small squares and hand around with drinks, or cut into bigger slices for a standing lunch. Either way, yum.

Prep time 30 mins, plus resting
Cook time 30–40 mins
Serves 6–8

2 cups (100 g) fresh spinach
　leaves
Zest and juice of 1 lemon
1 × quantity Ricotta filling
　(page 21)
1½ cups (195 g) peas, fresh or
　frozen, blanched then rinsed
　under cold water
½ handful parsley leaves
½ handful mint leaves
1 × quantity Shortcrust pastry
　(page 21), chilled
Plain (all-purpose) flour,
　for dusting
2 egg yolks
1 Tbsp cream
½ cup (45 g) grated parmesan,
　to finish

*'Almost everything' bagel
　seasoning*
3 Tbsp toasted white sesame
　seeds
2 Tbsp black sesame seeds
2 Tbsp sea salt
3 Tbsp fried shallots

Wash the spinach leaves well then transfer to a dry frying pan over medium heat. Cook for a few minutes, tossing as you go, to wilt the spinach right down into a soft clump of leaves. The residual moisture from washing should stop any of them from catching and burning.

Transfer to a chopping board and allow to cool for a few minutes.

For the 'almost everything' bagel seasoning, just combine the seeds and salt in a small jar and crumble in the fried shallots with your fingers. Mix well and set aside.

Add the lemon zest to the ricotta filling and whisk well. Finely chop the cooled spinach with 1 cup (130 g) of the peas, the parsley and mint. You could use a food processor to blitz this for a smoother texture, or just use a good knife for a rougher consistency. Either way, fold through the ricotta mixture and set aside while preparing the pastry.

Preheat the oven to 200°C (400°F).

Roll the chilled pastry out on a lightly floured benchtop so you have a large rectangle about 30 × 20 cm (12 × 8 inches). Transfer to a large baking tray lined with baking paper. Gently spoon the green ricotta mixture into the centre of the pastry, leaving a 4 cm (1½ inch) edge right around. Fold this down on each side to create a seal.

Whisk together the egg yolks and cream and brush along each side, then sprinkle with the seasoning. Pop in the oven for 30 minutes, or until the pastry is golden.

Meanwhile, for the topping, combine the remaining peas with the juice of your lemon, 1 tablespoon of the seasoning and the parmesan.

Once the tart is out of the oven and has cooled a little, sprinkle with the pea topping, slice and share.

Travel advice
Transport in a large container or tray, loosely wrapped in a tea towel, then sprinkle with the seasoning and parmesan before serving.

• *Pictured page 21*

Corn, goat's cheese, pickle and dill tarts

I love this flavour combination so much; the pickles, sliced quite thickly and baked with the rest, are such a flavour bomb with the buttery corn and creamy cheese. We have made these into small galettes here, but you could use a tart shell or muffin tins - whatever is easiest!

Prep time 30 mins, plus resting
Cook time 40 mins
Serves 4–6

1 Tbsp butter
3 cups (600 g) fresh corn kernels
  (from 3–4 ears)
1 × quantity Shortcrust pastry
  (page 21), chilled
Plain (all-purpose) flour,
  for dusting
1 handful dill, chopped
1 × quantity Ricotta filling
  (page 21)
150 g (5½ oz) goat's cheese,
  crumbled
1 cup (300 g) dill pickles, cut
  into 1 cm (½ inch) slices
2 egg yolks
1 Tbsp cream

Melt the butter in a heavy-based frying pan over medium–high heat and add the corn kernels. Cook, stirring often, for about 10 minutes, or until they are just beginning to catch and caramelise. Remove from the heat and set aside.

Preheat the oven to 200°C (400°F).

Roll out your chilled pastry on a lightly floured benchtop and cut into four to six rounds – I used a side plate with a 15 cm (6 inch) diameter. Transfer to a couple of trays lined with baking paper.

Add the dill to the ricotta filling and mix to combine. Place about 2 tablespoons of this in the middle of each pastry round. Top with a little goat's cheese, about 2 tablespoons of the cooked corn kernels and a few pickle slices.

Gently pinch the edges of your pastry together to form a crimped seal. Whisk the egg yolks and cream together and brush this mixture over the crimped edges.

Pop in the oven and cook for about 30 minutes, or until the tops are puffed and golden.

Travel advice
Allow the tarts to cool, then pile them into a container and wrap loosely with a tea towel. If you're going far, keep them chilled and let them come to room temperature before serving.

Small bites for a kids' party

Kids' birthday parties, in my opinion, are the perfect time to play a straight bat. There are enough variables and high emotions on the field already, so opting for crowd-pleasing party classics just makes sense, like the ones in this collection. They are all beloved favourites of kids and adults alike.

Just add a few big platters of cold watermelon slices and, of course, fairy bread – soft, buttered triangles of white bread liberally covered with sprinkles. A party essential!

Cook and party-thrower extraordinaire Laura Corcoran has shared her family's sausage roll and butterfly cake recipes with us here. Laura and her family live in Boorowa where she runs a small catering business and is mum to six little girls who love a party. She's the real deal: a modern country cook who does the classics with style and generosity.

Classic sausage rolls

This is a classic recipe - nothing fancy, but super tasty and everyone adores it. These quantities make loads of sausage rolls, but you'll want them (they freeze well). Thank you to Laura Corcoran's mother-in-law Anne for sharing her famous sausage rolls with us.

Prep time 30 mins
Cook time 30–40 mins
Makes 60

5 sheets frozen puff pastry
4 slices white bread, crusts
  removed
1 kg (2 lb 4 oz) minced (ground)
  sausage meat
1 brown onion, finely chopped
A good shake of dried
  mixed herbs
1 egg, beaten, for the egg wash

Preheat the oven to 220°C (425°F) and line two large baking trays with baking paper. Take the pastry out of the freezer to start thawing.

Put the bread in a mixing bowl and cover with warm water, then leave to soak for a couple of minutes. Once the bread has become soggy, use your hands to squeeze the water out and tear the soggy bread into small pieces.

In a large mixing bowl combine the bread, sausage meat, onion and herbs. Season with salt and pepper then get in there with your hands and give it a good mix.

Take a sheet of puff pastry and cut it in half. Place a log of sausage meat along each long edge, then carefully roll the sausage meat up in the pastry to create two long rolls. Cut each into six smaller rolls.

Repeat with the remaining pastry and sausage mix, then place the sausage rolls onto the trays and prick with a fork. Brush with the beaten egg and bake for 10 minutes, then reduce the oven to 180°C (350°F) and bake for another 20–30 minutes, or until cooked through and browned on top. Make sure you turn the trays around halfway through to ensure the sausage rolls bake evenly.

Serve with good old-fashioned tomato sauce or a chutney of choice.

Travel advice

My preference is to have these hot from the oven, so I cook them at the last minute and then transport them in an insulated bowl (a thick-walled bowl like a casserole dish wrapped in a tea towel will work at a pinch). Wrap a couple of heat packs in paper towel and place the rolls on top, then lid on and off you go. They're also good cold.

Tuna bites

I adore these little snacks. They're super easy to put together - more an assembly job than a recipe - and just really good and yummy. Like any simple recipe, you need to use the best ingredients you can, so a good salty, crunchy baguette and lovely tuna in oil would be great. Thank you, Laura, for sharing these with us. Their crunchy saltiness is a perfect foil to the cakes and treats at any kids' party!

Prep time 10 mins
Cook time NIL
Makes 6–8

½ cup (125 ml) crème fraîche
  or sour cream
¼ red onion, finely diced
2 Tbsp chopped baby
  cornichons, plus an extra
  ½ cup (75 g) baby cornichons,
  sliced lengthways
1 handful finely chopped
  flat-leaf parsley
Juice of ½ lemon
18–20 toasted or fresh baguette
  slices
400 g (14 oz) tuna in oil, or hot-
  smoked salmon, flaked

Mix the crème fraîche and onion together in a bowl.

Add the chopped cornichons, parsley and lemon juice, then season to taste with salt and pepper.

Spread a little of this mixture on the baguette slices, top with about 1 teaspoon of the flaked tuna, then top this with a thin slice of cornichon and secure with a toothpick.

Travel advice
Toast the baguette slices and make up the crème fraîche mixture then pack everything up and assemble on arrival. Or, if you're not travelling far (or at all), make these up at home and arrange on a nice plate to hand around with drinks.

Vanilla butterfly cakes

These pretty little cakes are favourites with all of Laura's kids. With everyone, actually. How could you not love a small vanilla sponge topped with whipped cream and strawberry jam? Thank you so much, Laura, for sharing this recipe, it's a delight.

Prep time 20 mins
Cook time 12–15 mins
Makes 12

175 g (6 oz) unsalted butter, at room temperature
¾ cup (165 g) caster (superfine) sugar
3 eggs, at room temperature
1 tsp vanilla extract
1½ cups (225 g) self-raising flour, sifted
½ cup (125 ml) full-cream milk
⅓ cup (110 g) strawberry jam

Whipped cream
300 ml (10½ fl oz) thick (double) cream
1 heaped tsp icing (confectioners') sugar, plus extra for dusting
1 scant tsp vanilla extract

Preheat the oven to 170°C (325°F) and line a 12-hole muffin tin with patty cases.

Place the butter in the bowl of a stand mixer fitted with the paddle attachment, or use a large bowl and an electric mixer, and beat for 2 minutes before gradually adding the sugar. Cream for a couple of minutes until pale and fluffy, scraping the side down as needed.

Reduce the speed to low and add the eggs, one at a time, mixing well between each addition. Now add the vanilla and mix for a few seconds to combine.

Add half of the flour and half of the milk, mix well, then repeat with the remaining flour and milk. Mix just until you have a smooth and cohesive batter.

Divide evenly between the patty cases and bake for 12–15 minutes, or until pale golden and cooked through when pierced with a skewer.

Cool the cupcakes on a wire rack.

Whip the cream to soft peaks, not too stiff, and fold in the teaspoon of icing sugar and the vanilla.

Once the cupcakes are completely cool, use a small, sharp knife to cut a little circle off the top of each one and then cut this little cake disc in half.

Add 1 teaspoon of jam to the hole, then dollop on a generous teaspoon of the whipped cream. Arrange the two pieces of cake you cut out on top in a 'butterfly' shape.

Dust with icing sugar.

Travel advice
It depends, as always, on how far you're travelling with these little cakes. But, as a general rule, if it's not around the corner, I'd take the whipped cream in an insulated cooler and assemble the cakes shortly before serving.

Italian-inspired dishes

Most small towns in Italy host a 'sagra' (festival) every year, usually in spring or summer, and usually in honour of an ingredient or dish special to their town or locality. I spent a few years living in Italy in my twenties, and I went to as many of these festivals as I could.

So in 2013, I was a bit excited to discover Griffith's Festa delle Salsicce (Festival of the Sausage), which marks the end of winter and welcomes spring.

We go most years, along with six hundred or so others who come together to celebrate this town's strong Italian food culture and compete in the home-made salami competition (I have even been a judge a few times – a big honour!). Every year, I'm impressed by how the festival volunteers come together to feed so many with such apparent ease and so much good food. And while the sausages are important, of course, it's also all about the sides for me! And for dessert? We head to our friends' nearby orchard for cake and bubbles – a perfect spring day.

Here are some ideas to bring an Italian 'sagra' vibe to your garden, street party or picnic.

Peperonata with sausage

We are in one-pot-wonder territory here, and this handy recipe joins two universally loved ingredients: sausage and potato, together with a garlicky, tomato sauce and multicoloured capsicums (peppers) for extra flavour and colour. It's equally excellent straight from the oven or at room temperature, and is a great switch-up from the classic potato salad. Leave the sausages out if you prefer a vegetarian option.

Prep time 30 mins
Cook time 1 hour 30 mins
Serves 4–6

500 g (1 lb 2 oz) potatoes, peeled and cut into thick French fries
⅓ cup (80 ml) olive oil
6 good-quality pork and fennel sausages
2 brown onions, thinly sliced
1 tsp fennel seeds
3 capsicums (peppers; ideally 1 yellow, 1 orange and 1 red), halved, seeded and sliced into 1 cm (½ inch) batons
3 garlic cloves, peeled and thinly sliced
2 Tbsp tomato paste (concentrated purée)
400 g (14 oz) tin whole peeled Italian tomatoes
1 handful fresh basil leaves

Bring a saucepan of water to the boil, add a good pinch of salt and cook the potatoes for 15 minutes or until just tender. Drain and set aside.

Heat half of the oil in a large ovenproof frying pan over medium–high heat and brown the sausages on all sides. Remove and set aside.

Add the remaining oil to the pan, reduce the heat to medium–low, add the onion and fennel seeds and cook for about 15 minutes or until completely softened. Now add the capsicum and garlic and sauté for about 15 minutes or until the capsicum has softened.

Preheat the oven to 180°C (350°F).

Add the tomato paste to the capsicum and onion mixture and season with salt and pepper. Squeeze the tinned whole tomatoes with your fingers to break them up and add to the pan. Fill the tin about three-quarters full of water, swirl it around, and tip that in, too. Stir well. Push the sausages and potato into the capsicum mixture, cover with a lid of foil and bake for 30–45 minutes, or until the sausages are cooked. Serve straight from the oven or warm, scattered with the basil leaves.

Travel advice

If you're planning on taking this some distance, ensure the dish is completely chilled before heading out. Transport it in an insulated ice box or cooler, then serve from there (it's delicious cold, too). If you're having this warm, be sure to eat it within 30–40 minutes of taking it out of the oven. If you have left the sausages out, you can relax this timing quite a lot.

Sformato

Essentially a baked cheese sauce with seasonal vegetables - I mean, how could you go wrong? Sformato in Italian usually refers to foods formed and cooked in a mould. And you could absolutely make this dish in six or eight small moulds or ramekins and turn them out in little dishes, perhaps topped with crumbled walnuts as a fancy starter. But for our party (or wherever you might like to take this), let's make one big sformato, fill it with peas and asparagus and share it at room temperature with crusty bread. Delicious.

Prep time 15 mins
Cook time 1 hour 15 mins
Serves 6–8

80 g (2¾ oz) unsalted butter
80 g (2¾ oz) plain (all-purpose) flour
3 cups (750 ml) full-cream milk
220 g (7¾ oz) grated parmesan or cheddar
A pinch of freshly grated nutmeg
1 cup (140 g) frozen or fresh peas
1 bunch asparagus, cut into 3 cm (1¼ inch) pieces
5 eggs

Preheat the oven to 180°C (350°F) and grease a 24 cm (9½ inch) springform cake tin or a small roasting tin or dish of your choice.

Melt the butter in a saucepan over medium heat and cook until it starts to foam. Add the flour and stir, cooking, for a few minutes or until you have a sandy, almost dry texture.

Add one-quarter of the milk and whisk until the mixture thickens. Gradually add the rest of the milk, whisking as you go. It will thicken up nicely after about 5 minutes.

Remove from the heat and stir in the cheese and nutmeg. Season well, then set aside to cool for 5 minutes.

Meanwhile, bring a small saucepan of water to the boil and blanch the peas and asparagus for 1 minute, then drain and rinse under cold water to help keep their lovely green colour.

Crack one of the eggs into the thickened white sauce and whisk to combine, then repeat with the remaining eggs, whisking them in one at a time.

Place your cake tin on a foil-lined tray (in case it leaks – mine sometimes does!) and pour in the cheesy white sauce. Sprinkle with the peas and asparagus. Bake for 50–60 minutes or until the sides have turned a lovely pale golden colour and it 'jiggles' just slightly in the middle when you give it a little shake.

Let cool to room temperature before cutting into wedges and serving.

Travel advice
Keep this chilled if travelling any distance, then bring it to room temperature before serving.

Note
Fold some puréed spinach through the cheesy white sauce before baking to turn this into a delicious bright green sformato, or add sliced cooked potatoes or any other seasonal vegetables you fancy.

Minestre (Greens and beans)

This is a simple, good dish of beans and greens. It's great at room temperature, at a picnic as a side dish, thinned out as a soup or piled atop crusty bread as a comforting supper. At last year's Festa delle Salsicce in Griffith, New South Wales, we sat with the lovely Mary Catanzariti, who told me how she would make a version of this for her children growing up, how she still makes it for them now when they need a taste of home. And how every cook makes theirs slightly differently. Here's my version.

Prep time 20 mins
Cook time 50–60 mins
Serves 6–8

¼ cup (60 ml) good-quality extra virgin olive oil
2 brown onions, finely chopped
4 garlic cloves, finely chopped
200 g (7 oz) pancetta, cut into small dice
2 cups (350 g) cooked white beans or 2 × 400 g (14 oz) tins white beans, drained and rinsed
2 cups (500 ml) chicken or vegetable stock
4 big handfuls kale, spinach or foraged greens of your choice, fairly finely chopped
1 parmesan rind (optional)
Grated parmesan, to serve
Lemon wedges (optional), to serve
Chilli oil (optional), to serve
A couple of handfuls of croutons (see Note)

Warm most of the olive oil in a large, heavy-based saucepan over low heat. Add the onion and cook for about 10 minutes, until soft and translucent. Add the garlic and pancetta and cook for 10 minutes more, stirring as you go so nothing catches and burns. Now add the beans and stir well to combine.

Pour in the stock, add the greens and parmesan rind, if using, and gently push them down into the stock to cook.

Season well and cook for 30–40 minutes, adding more stock or water as needed.

Serve drizzled with a little olive oil, a grating of parmesan and perhaps a squeeze of lemon and a little chilli oil. Thin out with more stock if you'd prefer this to be a soup.

Top with the croutons and serve at room temperature.

Travel advice

This is best warm or at room temperature, so perhaps leave home with it hot, in an insulated bowl or casserole dish wrapped in a towel to keep the heat in. Just before serving, drizzle with olive oil and extra cheese and top with the croutons.

Note

For the croutons, roughly chop half a loaf of crusty bread into small pieces. Toss the bread with olive oil and sea salt. Spread on a baking tray and roast in a 180°C (350°F) oven for about 15–20 minutes or until golden and crunchy. Let cool, then store in an airtight container for 1–2 days.

Gluten-free almond milk cheesecake

Annette Dinicola and her family run Mandolé Orchard just outside of Griffith, New South Wales, where they also produce the most beautiful, creamy almond milk. We visit them every Festa delle Salsicce, and at this time of year their orchard is like a fairyland of white blossoms. The perfect place for an afternoon tea among the trees. This is Annette's recipe. It's suitable for our gluten-free friends and can be made well in advance and left in the fridge till needed.

Prep time 20 mins, plus chilling
Cook time 10 mins
Serves 8

Cheesecake base
2 cups (320 g) whole natural
   almonds
50 g (1¾ oz) butter, melted
4 Tbsp caster (superfine) sugar

Cheesecake filling
2 × 250 g (9 oz) blocks cream
   cheese, at room temperature
¾ cup (165 g) caster (superfine)
   sugar
1 cup (250 ml) unsweetened
   almond milk, or milk of your
   choice
1 tsp vanilla essence
⅓ cup (80 ml) lemon juice
3 tsp gelatine powder dissolved
   in ¼ cup (60 ml) hot water

To finish
500 g (1 lb 2 oz) mixed berries
¼ cup (40 g) roughly chopped
   almonds

Preheat the oven to 180°C (350°F) and lightly grease a 25 cm (10 inch) loose-bottomed tart tin with approximately 3 cm (1¼ inch) high sides.

For the base, place the almonds in a food processor and blitz until you have a fine almond meal. Mix in the melted butter and the sugar, then firmly press the mixture into the tart tin, pressing it up the side in an even layer.

Bake for 10 minutes then remove from the oven and leave to cool while you make the filling.

Place the cream cheese and sugar in the bowl of a stand mixer fitted with the paddle attachment and beat for 2–3 minutes, or until light and smooth. (You can also use an electric mixer for this.) Add the milk, vanilla, lemon juice and gelatine mixture and beat for another 2 minutes until thoroughly combined.

Gently remove the tart shell from the tin, but leave it on the base for ease of movement, and transfer to a serving plate. Spoon in the filling and evenly smooth over the top. Place in the fridge to set for at least 3 hours, or overnight.

Before serving, arrange the berries on top and sprinkle with the chopped almonds.

Travel advice
Once set, this cheesecake will travel well in an insulated ice box or cooler.

Ideas for feasts (that can handle a bit of 'sitting' time)

- Green bean, pea, pasta and lemon salad (page 79)
- Slow-cooked capsicums with horseradish and balsamic (page 81)
- Burghul pilaf with roasted zucchini (page 120)
- Pearled barley, pickled onion, walnut and roasted cauliflower salad (page 129)
- Spicy confit chickpeas (page 160)
- Pearl couscous with roasted vegetables and goat's cheese (page 228)

Crostoli

I love crostoli. These fried pastry pillows dusted in sugar seem to be synonymous with festivals, feasts and village street parties in many parts of Italy, and they're a big weakness of mine. At Griffith's Festa delle Salsicce they're served for dessert and it's all you need after a big lunch. The festival volunteers spend an entire Sunday the week before making crostoli: rolling, frying and dusting in a well-oiled production line. Here is my recipe, inspired by theirs. It's not hard - essentially a sweet pasta dough that you roll thinly, fry and douse in sugar.

Prep time 35 mins, plus resting
Cook time 15 mins
Makes approx. 30

2 cups (300 g) plain (all-purpose) flour, plus extra for dusting
2 eggs
1 egg yolk
40 g (1½ oz) butter, softened
2 Tbsp brandy
1 tsp vanilla paste
1⅓ cups (295 g) caster (superfine) sugar, plus extra for dusting
1 vanilla pod
4 cups (1 litre) vegetable oil, for frying

If you are using a stand mixer fitted with the dough hook, place all the ingredients, except for 1 cup (220 g) of the caster sugar, the vanilla pod and vegetable oil, in the bowl, and knead for about 5 minutes, or until smooth and elastic (soft, not sticky). If working by hand, combine in a bowl until you have a rough dough, then turn out onto a benchtop and knead for about 5 minutes.

Divide the dough into four pieces, roll into balls, wrap in plastic wrap and leave to rest for 30 minutes.

Place the remaining caster sugar in a small bowl. Split the vanilla pod lengthways and scrape in the seeds. Using your fingers, work the vanilla into the sugar (it will smell so lovely), then set aside.

Pour the oil into a saucepan and line a baking tray with paper towel.

Roll the first ball of dough through a pasta machine, starting on the lowest/thickest setting. (You can lightly dust the dough with flour first if you think it might stick.) Fold it over and repeat until you have rolled and folded the dough at least six times, increasing the machine setting each time so you have a smooth and thin sheet of dough at the end.

Using a ravioli cutter or sharp knife, cut the dough into small rectangles, 4 × 8 cm (1½ × 3¼ inches). Cover with a damp tea towel and repeat with the remaining balls of dough. Here's when a second pair of hands comes in useful: one person continues to roll and cut and the other does the frying.

Meanwhile, heat the oil to frying point (if you have a cooking thermometer, that's 180°C/350°F, or test it by throwing in a small piece of dough; if it bubbles and rises immediately, it's ready). Grab some tongs and, ideally, a slotted spoon.

Cook the crostoli in batches, five to ten at a time (depending on how big your saucepan is), turning them with tongs or two forks as they cook, until golden in colour. Transfer to the lined tray to cool.

Once cool, transfer to a large, airtight container and dust with the vanilla caster sugar.

Travel advice
These last for a couple of weeks and do travel well. Put them in an airtight container to keep them crisp and protect them from breaking.

Treats for a cake stall or bake off

The Great Marburg Bake Off in southern Queensland is only in its fifth year, but this community-driven baking competition is already something special. This is mostly thanks to its driving force, chief organiser Erin Davis.

Erin has always been fascinated by show cookery; she's even trained to be a steward at the Ekka's (Queensland's annual agricultural show) highly contested cookery competition. She also believes that cake has magical powers to bring people together, as do I.

Bringing what feels like the entire village along for the ride, Erin created her own Bake Off and it's a joy to behold, from 9am when entries open and troupes of kindergarteners arrive bearing plates of decorated biscuits, to the final afternoon announcement of who won the chocolate cake category. When it's all over, the town decamps to the pub for an afterparty with live music, pink lemonade for the kids and pink gin and tonics for the grown-ups.

Here are some show-worthy recipes you might like to make and enter in your local competition, or just take to your next gathering.

Honey seed slice

This slice is just delicious, lasts for ages (a week on the bench, a couple in the fridge), is healthy-ish and free of gluten, dairy and nuts (handy). My friend, Elise, and her partner, Michael, run a bakery in Bondi, and this slice is a firm customer favourite. It's her recipe, and I now make it all the time. It's so good to have a big tin of this on hand in the kitchen for hungry kids, to take on car trips and pack in picnic baskets. Thanks, Elise!

Prep time 15 mins
Cook time 20 mins
Makes 16 bars

2⅓ cups (60 g) puffed brown rice
15 g (½ oz) cacao nibs
¼ cup (25 g) desiccated coconut
60 g (2 oz) pepitas (pumpkin seeds)
60 g (2 oz) sunflower seeds
⅓ cup (60 g) sultanas
60 g (2 oz) dried redcurrants
80 g (2¾ oz) chocolate chips
200 g (7 oz) honey
250 g (9 oz) tahini
1 tsp vanilla paste
½ tsp sea salt

Grease and line an 18 x 27 cm (7 x 10¾ inch) cake tin, or thereabouts, and preheat your oven to 170°C (325°F).

Mix the dry ingredients in a large bowl.

Combine the honey, tahini, vanilla and salt in a medium saucepan set over low heat and gently melt, stirring as you go, until you have a warm and smooth paste. Remove from the heat.

Wait 5 minutes for the honey mixture to cool a little (or the chocolate chips will melt), then tip into the bowl of dry ingredients.

I use my hands to gently mix and then scoop the mixture into the tin.

Smooth the mixture into an even layer then grab a glass, wet its base (so it doesn't stick) and use this to press the mixture down as firmly as you can.

Bake for 12 minutes, then leave to cool completely before cutting into squares or bars.

Travel advice
Transport in an airtight container or tin.

How to transform your cakes into slices
With a few small tweaks, most of the cakes in this book can easily be made into slices, which can be easier to cut and eat.

1. Swap your round cake tin for a rectangular roasting tin or cake tin, about 18 x 27 cm (7 x 10¾ inches). You want the batter to be around 4 cm (1½ inches) deep, with an extra 2 cm (¾ inch) of space for rising.
2. Reduce the cooking time (because the batter will be thinner). You can always check after 20–25 minutes by inserting a skewer in the middle of the slice.
3. Leave the slice to cool in the tin. Carefully cut it with a serrated knife before heading off.

The Great Marburg Bake Off chocolate cake

A simple, incredibly soft chocolate cake that is proud enough on its own but also happy to be iced with a buttercream (perhaps the one on page 148), or a fat layer of whipped cream and a pile of macerated strawberries. Many thanks to The Great Marburg Bake Off for sharing their competition recipe with us.

Prep time 10 mins
Cook time 40–45 mins
Serves 8–10

1¾ cups (260 g) self-raising flour, plus 1 Tbsp extra
¼ cup (30 g) cocoa powder
½ tsp bicarbonate of soda (baking soda)
¾ cup (165 g) caster (superfine) sugar
1 cup (250 ml) full-cream milk
2 eggs, lightly beaten
1 tsp vanilla essence
½ cup (125 g) butter, melted and cooled, plus extra for greasing

Preheat the oven to 180°C (350°F). Grease a 22 cm (8½ inch) round cake tin with butter. Tip the extra flour into the bottom of the tin and shake it to distribute it evenly, then tip the cake tin on its side and turn it so the flour evenly coats the side of the tin. Tip out any excess.

Sift the flour, cocoa powder and bicarbonate of soda together in a large bowl. Add the caster sugar and mix well. Combine the milk, egg and vanilla essence in a jug.

Add the milk mixture and cooled melted butter to the flour mixture and, using an electric mixer on low speed or a hand whisk, beat for 1 minute or until well combined. Pour the mixture into the tin and smooth the surface. Bake for 40–45 minutes, or until a skewer inserted in the middle of the cake comes out clean. Let it cool in the tin for 5 minutes, then turn onto a wire rack to cool completely.

Travel advice
Transport in an airtight container.

A few expert tips

If anyone can give us expert tips on baking, it's Maree Harvey. An accredited Queensland Country Women's Association Cookery Judge, Maree has been on the Brisbane Royal Agricultural Show Cookery Judging Panel since 2022. She has decades of experience in cooking, and entering and judging shows, so when she shares any baking advice, I sit up straight and listen. Thank you, Maree.

- If baking for show-judging, it's best to butter and flour your cake tins instead of lining them with baking paper. As the cake cooks, moisture is released, which can make the paper crinkle, giving the cake's edges and sides a crinkled, sometimes dented appearance that will lose you points.
- Don't overfill your measuring cup or spoon measures. Fill them, then level off with a knife. Overfilling can result in inaccurate measurements that can cause cracked cake tops and 'doming'. Be extra careful with bicarbonate of soda (baking soda); it can impart quite a strong flavour, and even a little more than the recipe suggests can adversely affect the cake's flavour.
- Avoid using a fan-forced setting in your oven for baking cakes. This can also contribute to cakes 'doming' or cracking. If your oven only has a fan-forced option, reducing the heat by 10–15°C (50–60°F) can help.
- To avoid holes in your cakes, bang the cake tin on the bench before putting it in the oven. This helps to remove any air pockets.
- Always read the recipe through to the end before you start. Follow it to the letter.

Peaches and cream custard sponge cake

Oh, but this is a lovely cake. There is just something about the colours, the smells, the peeling of peaches, and the whipped cream and happy faces when it's shared around. My family adores it and I find that making it makes me happy too. I like to use a slab-style cake tin, but a round one would also be fabulous. Here, we have a filling of poached peaches and softly whipped cream, but you could add any seasonal fruit, jam or even a lemon or passionfruit curd.

Prep time 30 mins, plus resting
Cook time 40–60 mins
Serves 10

6 eggs
¼ tsp cream of tartar
⅔ cup (150 g) caster (superfine) sugar
⅔ cup (100 g) plain (all-purpose) flour, plus extra for dusting
30 g (1 oz) custard powder
1 tsp baking powder
A pinch of sea salt
20 g (¾ oz) butter, melted, plus extra for greasing
¼ cup (60 ml) full-cream milk, warmed
1 tsp vanilla paste
Zest of 1 lemon
2 cups (500 ml) single (pure) cream
icing (confectioners') sugar, for dusting

Poached peaches
1 cup (220 g) sugar
1 vanilla pod, seeds scraped, or 1 tsp vanilla paste
6 ripe whole peaches

For the peaches, combine the sugar and vanilla (seeds and pod) with 4 cups (1 litre) water in a large saucepan over high heat and bring to the boil. Stir to dissolve the sugar, add the peaches and reduce the heat to low. Place a piece of baking paper on the surface of the water to stop the fruit from bobbing up and discolouring. Simmer for about 5 minutes or until the peaches are just tender. (The cooking time will depend on the ripeness and variety of the peaches, so test after 5 minutes.)

Remove the fruit from the poaching liquid and peel away the skin. It should come off quite easily by now, but if not, use a small sharp knife to help peel it off. Return the pan to the heat and boil the liquid for about 15 minutes until reduced by one-third. Let cool for 10 minutes then return the peeled peaches to the poaching liquid and leave to cool completely.

Meanwhile, preheat the oven to 170°C (325°F). Grease and line the base of an 18 × 26 cm (7 × 10½ inch) rectangular cake tin, or two 20 cm (8 inch) round cake tins, with baking paper. Grease the sides and lightly flour.

Separate the eggs and place the whites in the bowl of a stand mixer with the cream of tartar. (Alternatively, use a large bowl and an electric mixer.) Whisk until stiff peaks form, then add the sugar, 1 tablespoon at a time, then whisk for a few more minutes or until you have a glossy meringue. Turn the speed of your mixer down to low, then gradually add the egg yolks, whisking as you go. Continue whisking for another 10 seconds after adding the last yolk.

Sift the flour, custard powder, baking powder and sea salt together. Using the whisk attachment, but working by hand, gently incorporate the flour mixture into the egg and sugar mixture.

In a small jug, whisk together the butter, milk, vanilla and lemon zest, then, while still warm, gently whisk this into the batter, folding together gently until well incorporated.

Transfer the batter to your cake tin, or tins, and bake for 20 minutes if using two tins, or 30 minutes if using one tin. The cake is ready when a skewer inserted in the middle comes out clean and the top of the cake is pale golden.

Leave the cake to cool in the tin for about 5 minutes, then gently turn it out onto a wire rack.

While the cake is cooling, whip the cream to soft peaks. Remove three or four peaches from their poaching liquid and cut into small pieces. (Keep the remaining peaches to slice and serve with the cake, or have with yoghurt for breakfast the next day, perhaps.) Fold the chopped peaches into the cream.

Slice the cake in half and spread the peaches and cream mixture on the bottom half (or spread on one of the two round cakes), sandwich it with the other piece of cake and pop in the fridge for at least an hour. This makes it easier to cut, and the flavours settle in better. Bring the cake out of the fridge 20 minutes before serving, then dust with icing sugar at the last minute.

Travel advice

Transport the whipped cream, cake and peaches in separate containers in an insulated cooler, then assemble when you arrive.

Strawberry jam crumble slice

Melt the butter, mix everything together and you're done! This one couldn't be easier, but the key thing is to let it cool completely in the fridge before slicing or it will fall apart. Swap the jam with marmalade if you prefer.

Prep time 10 mins
Cook time 1 hour 5 mins
Makes approx. 20 small squares

175 g (6 oz) unsalted butter, plus extra for greasing
½ cup (110 g) brown sugar
1 tsp vanilla paste
A pinch of salt
1 cup (100 g) rolled oats
½ cup (45 g) desiccated coconut
180 g (6½ oz) plain (all-purpose) flour
1 cup (320 g) strawberry jam, or jam of your choice

Start by browning the butter. Place the butter in a small saucepan over medium heat and melt, stirring as you go. Continue cooking until it begins to brown, about 5–6 minutes, then pour into a bowl or jug and leave to cool for 5 minutes.

Preheat the oven to 160°C (315°F) and grease and line a 20 cm (8 inch) square slice tin.

Combine the cooled brown butter, sugar, vanilla, salt, oats, coconut and flour in a bowl. Mix together with your hands until you have a crumbly dough. Press half of this mixture into the base of your lined tin. Spread this with the jam and crumble the remaining dry mixture over it.

Bake for 1 hour, or until the top is golden brown. Remove from the oven and allow to cool completely before chilling in the fridge. Once well chilled, slice into bars. If you try to slice this while still warm it will crumble and collapse. It will still be tasty, but not so much in 'bar' form.

Travel advice
Once fully cooled, transport these bars in a tin or airtight container.

A family barbecue

Michelle Lim is a seriously wonderful cook. The recipes on the next few pages are all hers and all sing with the flavours of her Filipino childhood. I'm so happy and appreciative to be sharing them here.

Michelle moved to Australia in 2011, after meeting her now-husband Tom who was working in her home town of Dumaguete in the Philippines. They eventually settled in the town of Boorowa with their two children, and together have taken on the renovation of a wonderful old house full of eclectic art. On the day we visited, the most incredible smells wafted from the family's kitchen. Their veggie garden is an inspiration: rows upon rows of herbs, vegetables and fruit trees. They grow to feed themselves and share with friends.

This feast was incredibly tasty, generous, colourful and shareable – the kind of food we all want to load our table with. Thank you, Michelle.

Depending on where, and how big, your local supermarket is, and whether you can get to a specialty Asian grocery store, some of these ingredients might be hard to find. Michelle lives a couple of hours from Canberra, where her favourite Filipino ingredients can be found at specialty shops. You can always jump online to order what's needed (I do this at a pinch). I have suggested alternatives wherever possible as well.

Menu

Feast.

Pork belly sisig

Since Michelle shared this recipe with me, I've adopted this sisig as a go-to when catering for big groups. It is just so delicious and easy. Everything can be done well in advance, and then you just cook the poached pork belly on site and dunk it into that crazy good sauce - the result is unbelievably tasty. Serve with rice or flatbreads. Trust me, it's an absolute winner.

Prep time 20 mins
Cook time 2 hours 20 minutes
Serves 6–8

2 kg (4 lb 8 oz) piece pork belly

Brine
2 red onions, finely chopped
6 garlic cloves, roughly chopped
5 bay leaves
1 Tbsp black peppercorns
½ cup (125 ml) soy sauce
⅓ cup (80 ml) coconut vinegar,
　or white vinegar if you can't
　find it
2 bird's eye chillies, finely
　chopped (seeded, if you want
　to reduce the heat)

Dipping sauce
1 cup (250 ml) soy sauce
¾ cup (185 ml) sugarcane juice,
　or rice vinegar
1 red onion, finely sliced
1 red chilli, finely sliced
1 green chilli, finely chopped
5 cumquats, halved, or limes
　if they're not in season

Start this recipe the day before you want to serve it. Place the pork belly in a large saucepan or stockpot. Add all the brine ingredients and enough water to just cover the pork. Place over medium heat and bring to a simmer, then reduce the heat to medium–low and simmer for 2 hours or until the meat is tender. Refrigerate in the brine overnight.

The next day, make the dipping sauce by combining all the ingredients in a bowl.

When you're ready to cook the pork, heat a charcoal barbecue until the coals are smoking and pour the dipping sauce into a large, high-sided serving tray.

Remove the pork from the brine. Grill the meat for 15–20 minutes, turning it halfway so it is cooked through and caramelised on both sides. If you don't have a charcoal barbecue, you can just heat a regular one to high and cook for a similar time, turning halfway, until cooked through. You won't get that great smoky flavour, but it'll still be super good. I've also shoved this into our pizza oven when it was very hot (around 300°C/570°F), and it caramelised and cooked beautifully in minutes.

Either way, remove the pork from the heat, chop it into big chunks and dunk it straight into the tray of dipping sauce. Serve immediately.

Travel advice
If you're taking this to a gathering, brine the pork overnight as per the recipe. Remove the pork from the brine and tightly wrap with plastic wrap. Make the dipping sauce in a big jar. Transport the pork and sauce in an insulated cooler. Fire up the charcoal (or gas) barbecue and cook as above.

Lamb kaldereta

Michelle's kaldereta recipe transports her back to her childhood in the Philippines, where she remembers her family making this dish for every special occasion. It's a tomato-based stew with Spanish origins and it's incredibly tasty. As a child, Michelle remembers her family breeding goats especially for this dish. These days, she also makes it with lamb, and now I do, too.

Prep time 10 mins
Cook time 2 hours 30 mins
Serves 6–8

⅓ cup (80 ml) olive oil
2 kg (4 lb 8 oz) boneless lamb shoulder, diced
2 brown onions, finely diced
6 garlic cloves, finely diced
1 kg (2 lb 4 oz) pack Filipino-style tomato sauce (see Notes)
85 g (3 oz) tin liver spread (optional; see Notes)
4 carrots, trimmed, peeled and cut into thirds
5 baby potatoes, scrubbed and halved
½ red capsicum (pepper), thinly sliced
½ green capsicum (pepper), thinly sliced
½ yellow capsicum (pepper), thinly sliced
1 cup (160 g) kalamata olives (pitted or not, up to you), rinsed
Cooked rice, to serve

Heat 3 tablespoons of the olive oil in a large, heavy-based casserole dish over medium–high heat. Sear the lamb on all sides then set aside. Reduce the heat to medium, add the remaining oil and cook the onion until translucent, about 7 minutes, then add the garlic and cook for another few minutes.

Add the tomato sauce and liver spread, if using, along with ½ cup (125 ml) water. Stir well, then bring to a simmer before reducing the heat to low. Return the lamb to the casserole dish and cook, uncovered, for about 1 hour. Add the carrots and potatoes and cook over low heat for a further hour, or until the potatoes are cooked through and the lamb is tender. Add the capsicum and olives and cook for another 15–20 minutes. Season well with salt and pepper, then serve warm with rice.

Travel advice
This really needs to be served hot so make sure it's piping when you leave home, transport in an insulated container, casserole dish or your slow-cooker bowl and wrap in towels to keep in as much heat as possible. Reheat on arrival if needed.

Notes
- *Filipino-style tomato sauce is slightly sweet and acidic. It is available at many supermarkets, but if you can't find it at yours, use two 400 ml (14 fl oz) jars of tomato passata (puréed tomatoes) with 2 teaspoons brown sugar and 2 tablespoons apple cider vinegar.*
- *Liver spread can be compared to a French-style pâté, but spicier. It is considered the 'secret' ingredient for a proper kaldereta, but you can leave it out if you prefer. It's available from specialty Asian grocers and some supermarkets.*

Pandan chicken

Michelle's little chicken rolls are such a great thing to take to and share at any gathering; they're good cold or straight off the barbecue, and the pandan leaves give a lovely flavour to the chicken. They're definitely worth seeking out at your nearest Asian grocery store.

Prep time 20 mins, plus
  overnight resting
Cook time 35–40 mins
Serves 6–8

800 g (1 lb 12 oz) boneless,
  skinless chicken thighs
2 tsp sea salt
1 tsp freshly ground black pepper
¼ cup (60 ml) olive oil
6–8 fresh pandan leaves

Cut the chicken thighs in half lengthways. Season well with the salt and pepper and rub with half of the olive oil. Roll the chicken up in the pandan leaves to make little parcels, ensuring they are tightly bound, then secure each with a toothpick. Refrigerate overnight.

Preheat the oven to 120°C (235°F).

Heat the remaining olive oil in a frying pan and fry the pandan-wrapped chicken for 2–3 minutes on each side or until golden. Transfer to a roasting tin and continue cooking in the oven for 30 minutes or until cooked through (open one up to check).

Travel advice
These are delicious hot or cold. If going for the former, assemble the rolls at home and keep thoroughly chilled, then barbecue on arrival. If the latter, cook the rolls at home, then chill completely and keep chilled right up until serving.

Leche flan (Caramel custard)

It makes sense to make Michelle's flan and pavlova together because they use nearly all the eggs called for in both recipes, except for two egg whites. Also, they just seem to scream 'this is a party'.

Prep time 10 mins
Cook time 50 mins
Serves 8–10

2 Tbsp caster (superfine) sugar
10 egg yolks
400 g (14 oz) tin condensed milk
400 ml (14 fl oz) tin evaporated milk
1 tsp vanilla essence

If you have a proper flan tin, a llanera, then now's the time to use it. If you don't, just make the caramel separately then continue the recipe with a shallow 4-cup (1-litre) capacity dish.

Place 1 tablespoon of the sugar in your llanera or a small saucepan over medium heat. Once the sugar has melted, you can set it aside or, if using the saucepan, pour it into your shallow dish.

Mix the egg yolks, condensed milk, evaporated milk, vanilla and remaining sugar in a bowl and stir together very gently, trying not to create bubbles.

Sieve the mixture twice, then gently pour over the melted sugar so it comes about three-quarters of the way up the side of your llanera or dish.

Cover the dish with foil, then place in the basket of a large steamer. (If you don't have a steamer, or one big enough to hold your dish, place the dish in a large roasting tin filled halfway with water and cook in a 150°C/300°F oven for 40 minutes, or until a skewer inserted in the middle comes out clean.) Cover with the steamer lid and set atop a saucepan of barely simmering water over very low heat; you don't want it boiling or the eggs will curdle. Steam for 40 minutes or until a skewer inserted in the middle comes out clean.

Refrigerate to chill completely, then turn out onto a serving platter when ready to go.

Travel advice
Transport and serve nicely chilled.

Pavlova

What is a gathering without a pavlova? And this is a glorious big one. Top with whatever seasonal fruit you prefer. Michelle used a mixture of strawberries, golden kiwi fruit, banana and passionfruit.

Prep time 20 mins
Cook time 1 hour 20 mins
Serves 8–10

8 egg whites
2 cups (440 g) caster (superfine) sugar
4 Tbsp cornflour (cornstarch)
4 tsp white vinegar
1 cup (250 ml) single (pure) cream, freshly whipped
3 cups (450 g) seasonal fruit

Preheat the oven to 150°C (300°F) and line a large baking tray with baking paper. Trace about a 25 cm (10 inch) diameter circle onto the paper with a pencil, then flip it over so that the pencil won't come in contact with the meringue but so you can still see the line.

Place the egg whites in a stand mixer fitted with the whisk attachment, or use a large bowl and an electric mixer, and whisk the whites to soft peaks. Gradually add the sugar, a little at a time, until it is all incorporated. Whisk for 3 minutes, or until a little mixture rubbed between your fingertips no longer feels grainy. Gently fold in the cornflour and vinegar.

Transfer the meringue to your baking tray and try to keep it within your traced circle. Use a spatula to draw up the sides of the meringue to create edges of an even height all the way around.

Reduce the oven to 120°C (235°F) and bake for 1 hour and 20 minutes. Turn the oven off and wedge a wooden spoon inside the oven door to hold it slightly ajar. Leave the meringue to cool completely in the oven.

When you're ready to serve, spread the pavlova with the whipped cream and top with the fruit.

Travel advice
The 'undressed' pavlova will keep for a few days in an airtight container, so transport it as is. Whip the cream and cut up the fruit, then transport chilled in a cooler and assemble the pavlova just before serving.

Buko pandan (Young coconut dessert)

This delicately flavoured dessert is just perfect to make and share after dinner on a warm night. When we ate at Michelle's she had prepared these in advance and then served them perched atop a bed of ice on a big tray. It looked great and was the perfect way to keep them cold as part of a dessert spread.

Prep time 10 mins, plus chilling
Cook time 5 mins
Serves 6–8

1 box (95 g) pandan jelly (see Notes)
3 cups (240 g) grated young coconut (see Notes)
400 g (14 oz) tin condensed milk
400 ml (14 fl oz) tin evaporated milk
A few drops of pandan essence (see Notes)
3 titanium-strength gelatine leaves
1 cup (250 ml) single (pure) cream
Mint leaves, to serve

Make the pandan jelly according to the packet instructions. Pour into a 20 × 20 cm (8 × 8 inch) square tin and leave to set in the fridge for 6 hours or until firm.

Mix the grated coconut, condensed milk and evaporated milk in a bowl until well combined. Drop in the pandan essence, a little at a time, until you have a pale green colour. Mix well.

Soak the gelatine leaves in cold water for a few minutes.

Heat the cream in a small saucepan until just at boiling point, then remove from the heat. Squeeze the water from the gelatine and whisk the softened leaves into the hot cream until completely dissolved. Stir this mixture into the coconut mixture, then divide between small glass bowls or place in one large bowl and refrigerate for at least 6 hours, or until set.

Cut the pandan jelly into small cubes and dot across the top of the pandan desserts. Finish with a mint leaf or two and serve chilled.

Travel advice
You could do as Michelle did and serve these desserts on a bed of ice, or keep them in the fridge or an insulated cooler right up until dessert. If making this for a picnic, I would do so in one large plastic container then scoop out into little cups and decorate with the jelly and mint. It's just so much easier to transport than lots of individual glasses.

Notes
- *Pandan essence and jelly should be available at Asian grocers. If you can't find the jelly, use unflavoured jelly crystals and add a few drops of green food colouring and pandan essence. Or skip the jelly on top – it will still be completely delicious without it.*
- *You can buy grated young coconut in the fridge/freezer section of most Asian grocers. Defrost before using.*

Crinkle biscuits

Michelle tells me these biscuits were always the first to go at any sports day, birthday or school party; they're crunchy on the outside and fudgy in the middle. Her family would always take them to parties when she lived in the Philippines, and I'm so happy to have this recipe now so that I can do the same. Thank you, Michelle.

Prep time 20 mins, plus resting
Cook time 15 mins
Makes 20–30

½ cup (125 g) unsalted butter, at room temperature
1¼ cups (275 g) caster (superfine) sugar
⅔ cup (75 g) cocoa powder
1 Tbsp vanilla essence
75 g (2¾ oz) dark chocolate (minimum 70% cocoa), melted
4 eggs
2 cups (300 g) plain (all-purpose) flour
1 tsp baking powder
1 cup (125 g) icing (confectioners') sugar

Combine the butter and caster sugar in the bowl of a stand mixer fitted with the whisk attachment, or you can use a large bowl and an electric mixer. Beat until pale and creamy, about 2–3 minutes.

Add the cocoa powder, vanilla and melted chocolate and beat for another minute.

Add the eggs, one at a time, beating well between each addition and scraping down the side of the bowl as you go if necessary.

Swap to the paddle attachment, fold in the flour and baking powder, and gently mix until well combined.

Cover the bowl and refrigerate for at least 4 hours, or overnight.

When ready to bake, preheat the oven to 180°C (350°F) and line two trays with baking paper. Place the icing sugar in a small bowl. Scoop the dough into balls about the size of an unshelled walnut, then roll each ball in the icing sugar until fully coated. Place on the trays a few centimetres (about ¾ inch) apart to allow for spreading.

Bake for 12 minutes, or until puffed and smelling amazing.

Transfer to a wire rack to cool, then store in an airtight container for up to a week.

Travel advice
Store and transport these in an airtight container or jar.

Summer.

Late dinners on balmy evenings, big gatherings in the shade on stinking-hot days, street parties and family lunches; summer is peak 'bring a plate' season. See you out there with a cooler bag and an umbrella!

Salads that won't wilt in the heat

Whether it's Christmas, New Year or any summer celebration, and it's hot outside, it's possible the food might be sitting in a warm spot for some time, so we need to play it safe with our ingredients. We want olive oil-based dressings, no dairy (or only last-minute dairy additions), no mayo, lots of crunch, and vegetables that will hold their shape and texture. We want raw veggies cut small and dressed big, roasted veggies marinated in oil, big colours and lots of flavour. These salads check all of these boxes and are my go-tos when I'm asked to bring something to a summery lunch, but I also reach for them year-round, with some seasonal substitutions. They're all special enough for a celebration feast, but easy enough for a casual beach barbecue.

Crunchy broccoli 'spoon' salad

Bright, crunchy, packed with big flavours and very healthy, this salad ticks all the boxes. Plus, it sits beautifully at room temperature (within reason) as long as you add the cheese at the last minute. A good chopped 'spoon' salad is an underrated thing - so handy when you're standing up at a party and only have one hand free to eat with. This salad is excellent as is, but if you want to, add a few chopped hard-boiled eggs, some hot-smoked salmon or tuna, or perhaps some poached chicken. If you haven't tried raw broccoli, trust me, it's really good!

Prep time 15 mins, plus softening
Cook time 10 mins
Serves 6 as a side, 3–4 as a main

⅓ cup (55 g) whole almonds
2 Tbsp tamari
1 head broccoli
6 dates, stones removed, finely chopped
¼ cup (60 ml) extra virgin olive oil
Zest and juice of 2 lemons (about 100 ml/3½ fl oz)
1 tsp honey
1 large garlic clove, finely chopped
A pinch of chilli flakes, to taste
1 Tbsp dijon mustard
¾ cup (150 g) tri-colour quinoa, rinsed and cooked according to the packet instructions
120 g (4¼ oz) mature cheddar, cut into small cubes

Place the almonds and tamari in a dry frying pan and cook over medium heat, tossing often, for about 10 minutes or until the almonds look dry and smell aromatic. Let the nuts cool, then roughly chop and set aside.

Finely chop the broccoli florets and peel and finely chop the stem. Place in a large bowl with the dates and chopped almonds.

For the dressing, combine the olive oil, lemon zest and juice, honey, garlic, chilli, some salt and pepper and the mustard in a small jar and shake well. Pour it over the broccoli, add the quinoa and toss to combine. Set your salad aside for at least 30 minutes before serving so that the dressing can 'soften' the broccoli.

Toss through the cheddar and serve.

Travel advice

This salad travels so well and really doesn't mind being left out at room temperature for some time. In fact, it gets better with time, within reason – just make sure you add the cheese right before serving.

Washing salads

Here are a few tips for making a simple green salad to transport on a warm day.

1. Fill a bowl or the sink with cold water. Plunge in your greens and leave to sit for a minute or so to allow any grit to sink to the bottom.
2. Remove and spin or shake as dry as you can.
3. Lay a couple of tea towels on your benchtop and arrange your greens across them. Gently roll into two sausages and place in the fridge or an insulated ice box or cooler.
4. When you're ready to serve, simply unwrap and tip the leaves straight into your salad bowl, ready to dress.

Mango, macadamia nut and cabbage salad

This is the salad my brother Will makes for us at Christmas, and it's wonderful, especially alongside a freshly glazed ham (see page 197). The macadamia nut and mango combination is divine, and the whole salad just sings of summer. Swap out the macadamia nuts for almonds or walnuts if you prefer, and add in any other crunchy, fresh vegetables you have on hand.

Prep time 15 mins
Cook time 10 mins
Serves 6 as a side

½ cup (110 g) sugar
1 tsp sea salt
1½ cups (230 g) macadamia nuts
½ tsp chilli flakes
½ green cabbage, finely shredded
½ red cabbage, finely shredded
1 red capsicum (pepper), halved, seeded and finely sliced
1 handful parsley leaves, roughly chopped
1 handful mint leaves, roughly chopped
2 mangoes, peeled, stones removed, flesh thinly sliced
3 Tbsp olive oil
Zest and juice of 1 lime

Line a baking tray with baking paper and heat a small, heavy-based saucepan over medium heat. Add the sugar, salt and macadamia nuts to the pan and cook, stirring often, for about 10 minutes or until the nuts are coated in a golden caramel. Add the chilli flakes, stir, then spread the nuts on your tray to cool completely.

Combine the cabbage, capsicum, herbs, mango and cooled nuts in a large bowl. Pour in the olive oil and lime juice and sprinkle in the zest. Get your clean hands in there and mix well.

Travel advice
Prepare the salad up to the point of adding the herbs, mango, nuts and dressing. Keep all of the elements chilled and separate, and assemble right before serving.

Below: Charred cabbage salad with butterbeans
Top right: Green bean, pea, pasta and lemon salad

Charred cabbage salad with butterbeans

This is such a good, substantial salad* for a picnic or any shared meal. It's delicious hot or at room temperature, and don't worry if the wedges fall apart while cooking - they'll still taste and look the goods. If you fancy making this as a main dish, I'd smear a layer of yoghurt on the bottom of each plate and pile the cabbage and beans on top.
Purists might argue this isn't quite a salad, more of a vegetable dish. Either way, it's delish!

Prep time 10 mins
Cook time 20 mins
Serves 6 as a side, 3–4 as a main

100 ml (3½ fl oz) olive oil, plus extra for drizzling
400 g (14 oz) tin butterbeans, drained and rinsed
2 lemons
½ savoy cabbage, cut into wedges
40 g (1½ oz) butter, cubed
1 handful dill leaves
2 Tbsp dukkah (see page 113)

Heat 3 tablespoons of the oil in a large frying pan over medium–high heat and fry the beans for a few minutes, turning to crisp all sides. Remove from the pan and squeeze the juice of 1 lemon over the beans.

Add the remaining oil to the pan and then add the cabbage wedges. Cook them for about 5 minutes on each side or until browned all over. Add the butter, the zest of your remaining lemon and ¼ cup (60 ml) water. Cover with a lid (or a layer of foil), then reduce the heat to low and cook for a further 5 minutes or until the cabbage is completely soft.

Remove from the heat and sprinkle the beans, dill and dukkah over the cabbage. Finish with some salt and pepper to taste, a good squeeze of the zested lemon and a final drizzle of olive oil.

Travel advice
This travels beautifully – just keep the dill, dukkah and lemon juice aside and add at the end. Store in an airtight container and serve straight from that. It's best at room temperature (within reason).

Green bean, pea, pasta and lemon salad

The key here is using the best, sturdiest pasta you can get and only cooking till al dente so it holds its shape. If I'm making this for dinner on a summer's evening, I might also shred in a barbecued chook.

Prep time 15 mins
Cook time 20 mins
Serves 6 as a side, 3–4 as a main

1 tsp salt
400 g (14 oz) green beans
1 cup (130 g) frozen peas
500 g (1 lb 2 oz) small pasta, such as conchiglie
¼ cup (60 ml) olive oil
Zest and juice of 2 lemons
3 garlic cloves, finely chopped
¼ cup (50 g) capers, drained
½ cup (75 g) sun-dried tomatoes, roughly chopped
½ cup (80 g) pine nuts, toasted
1 handful parsley leaves, roughly chopped
½ cup (65 g) feta cheese, crumbled

Bring a large pot of water to the boil and add the salt. Cook the green beans and peas for 1 minute, then remove with a slotted spoon and run under cold water in a colander. Bring the water back to the boil, add the pasta and cook until al dente. Drain and rinse under cold running water. Chop the blanched beans into pieces about 3–4 cm (1¼–1½ inches).

Heat the olive oil in a small frying pan over medium–high heat. Add the lemon zest, garlic, capers and sun-dried tomatoes and cook, stirring often, for 10 minutes.

Put the pasta in a large bowl. Tip in the hot oil mixture, then add the juice from the zested lemons, the beans, peas and pine nuts. Mix to combine well. Store in the fridge and, just before serving, toss through the parsley and feta.

Travel advice
This salad gets better with time. If you are travelling or leaving it out, just add the feta and herbs at the last minute.

Big flavour dressing ♡

Slow-cooked capsicums with horseradish and balsamic

There is a lot of flavour going on here for such a simple recipe. It's such a winner not only to bring as a salad (with bread), but also as a bed for roasted meats, as a bruschetta topping, or perhaps tossed through pasta or layered into a crazy good lasagne. In short, please consider making double.

Prep time 15 mins
Cook time 1 hour 15 mins
Serves 4–6 as a side

4 red capsicums (peppers), halved, seeds
   and membrane removed, then quartered
1 tsp sea salt
1 tsp freshly ground black pepper
4 thyme sprigs
3 Tbsp olive oil
2 Tbsp balsamic vinegar
1 tsp freshly grated horseradish,
   or 2 Tbsp horseradish cream

Preheat the oven to 160°C (315°F).
   Place the capsicums in an ovenproof dish, making sure they fit fairly snugly. Sprinkle in the salt, pepper and thyme and pour in ¼ cup (60 ml) water. Cover with a lid or foil and bake for 45 minutes. Remove the cover, toss everything around and return to the oven for 30 minutes or until the capsicums are completely soft and have shrunk down quite a bit.
   While still warm, drizzle with the olive oil and balsamic and toss well. At this point, the dish can sit happily at room temperature for a few hours, then, just before serving, grate the horseradish over it or dollop on the horseradish cream.

Travel advice
This one is okay to leave out at room temperature for a couple of hours, and it will taste better, too. Transport in a tight container as there are lots of juices here that can seep and stain if yours has a dodgy lid. Speaking from experience…

Tomato, olive and big crouton salad

Use the best-quality tomatoes you can find for this salad, and please start with them at room temperature. Salting the tomatoes helps to draw out moisture, creating a 'sauce' to build on. Add the croutons and basil just before serving, or just pile this mixture onto a slice of sourdough.

Prep time 15 mins, plus soaking
Cook time 15–20 mins
Serves 6 as a side

½ cup (60 g) black olives, pitted
5–6 large heirloom tomatoes, or any good, ripe
   tomatoes, cut into eighths, at room temperature
¼ tsp sugar, or just a pinch if your tomatoes are
   super sweet
1 Tbsp sea salt
½ loaf stale or day-old sourdough bread or baguette
¼ cup (60 ml) olive oil, plus extra for drizzling
2 Tbsp red wine vinegar
2 garlic cloves, finely chopped
½ cup (25 g) basil leaves

Rinse the olives under warm water and leave to soak in cold water for up to an hour. While the olives are soaking, toss the tomatoes, sugar and salt in a separate bowl and leave to sit for an hour. The sugar and salt will draw out moisture from the tomatoes, leaving you with a puddle of delicious sauce.
   Drain, rinse and place the olives in your salad bowl.
   Preheat the oven to 200°C (400°F) and tear the bread into large chunks. Place on a baking tray, drizzle with oil and bake for 15–20 minutes or until golden and crunchy.
   Tip your juicy tomatoes into the salad bowl with the olives and add the oil, vinegar, garlic and basil. Gently toss with your fingers to combine, then add the croutons, mix again and serve.

Travel advice
Transport the basil and croutons in separate containers to the salad. This one is okay to travel at room temperature.

Something for morning tea

I met some girlfriends for a Sunday morning bushwalk recently and had some plum cake (see page 86) in a basket with a thermos of coffee ready to share on our return. It was such a lovely treat – not too sweet, and perfect sustenance after hiking up a big hill. You could do the same with the little granola jars (see page 89), but in a cooler bag, and/or perhaps pack up Kristine's rhubarb crumble (see page 85) with a few small bowls and spoons.

If this sounds at all like a fiddle, please trust me that the packing is the work of minutes and the delight you'll feel and receive on producing such a lovely morning tea outstrips any effort in creating it by about 1000 per cent.

Whether it's al fresco on a walking picnic or at a friend's house on a sunny Saturday, I hope you enjoy these recipes one morning soon.

Rhubarb and marzipan crumble

Both marzipan and rhubarb are beloved ingredients in designer Kristine Lindbjerg Hansen's native Denmark, and she's even now growing almonds and rhubarb on the farm she shares with her husband and two sons near Capertee, a couple of hours north-west of Sydney. I'd happily take this to a picnic to share at room temperature or bring it out at a fancy dinner party to serve hot with cold ice cream. It's just so light and lovely. Thank you, Kristine, for sharing this recipe with us.

Prep time 15 mins
Cook time 40 mins
Serves 6–8

1 kg (2 lb 4 oz) rhubarb, trimmed and stalks cut into small cubes
⅓ cup (75 g) caster (superfine) sugar
1 vanilla pod, split lengthways and seeds scraped
200 g (7 oz) marzipan, crumbled
25 g (1 oz) butter, cubed
1 cup (100 g) almond meal
vanilla ice cream or cream, to serve

Preheat the oven to 200°C (400°F).

Place the rhubarb in a shallow baking dish and scatter the sugar over it. Add the vanilla seeds and throw in the pod halves, then toss together with your fingers.

Bake for about 20 minutes, or until the rhubarb has softened but still holds its shape. Remove the vanilla pod.

Crumble the marzipan over the rhubarb, dot the top with the butter and sprinkle with the almond meal.

Return to the oven for a further 20 minutes, or until the top of the crumble is pale golden.

Serve with vanilla ice cream or cream.

Travel advice

I'd transport this in the dish you made it in, covered and tucked into a basket or tray where it won't jiggle around. Don't worry too much about keeping it chilled. This will be lovely at room temperature.

Czech yeasted plum cake

'Back home in Czech,' my friend Vladka says, 'everyone has a fruit tree in their garden, and everyone has eggs, sugar, butter and flour in their kitchen. So, we cook with what we have and with what is in season.' Vladka and I first connected over our love of elderflowers, many of which grow on our farm. We then moved on to cake and here we are, in her kitchen, with a basket of damson plums picked from a tree on the road that connects our houses, making this sweet plum cake. It's a recipe from her childhood, and one I now make often and love, too.

Prep time 30 mins, plus proving
Cook time 30–35 mins
Serves 8–10

Dough
8 g (¼ oz) dry yeast
1 cup (250 ml) lukewarm
  full-cream milk
60 g (2 oz) caster (superfine)
  sugar
A pinch of salt
3⅓ cups (500 g) pastry flour
  (see Note), plus extra for
  dusting
2 Tbsp melted butter, cooled
1 egg

Drobenka (Crumb)
1 cup (150 g) plain (all-purpose)
  flour
½ cup (125 g) butter, cubed
½ cup (110 g) caster (superfine)
  sugar
1 tsp ground cinnamon
A pinch of salt

Plums
1 kg (2 lb 4 oz) plums, halved,
  stones removed

For the dough, combine the yeast and milk in the bowl of a stand mixer fitted with the dough hook attachment and mix well. Set aside in a warm place for 5 minutes or until bubbles appear on the surface.

Add the sugar, salt, flour, butter and egg and knead for 1 minute on high, then reduce the speed to medium and mix for another 4 minutes, or until the dough comes away from the side of the bowl and feels soft and elastic. You can do the final minute or so by hand on the bench if you prefer.

Remove the dough and lightly oil the bowl, then return the dough to the bowl and cover with a tea towel. Leave to rise at room temperature for about an hour, or until doubled in size.

Meanwhile, prepare the crumb. Combine all the ingredients in a small bowl and mix together with your fingertips.

Preheat the oven to 180°C (350°F).

Turn the dough out onto a lightly floured benchtop and gently roll into a rectangle around 30 × 40 cm (12 × 16 inches), or to fit a large baking tray.

Line your tray with baking paper and gently transfer the dough on top. Leave for another 30 minutes.

Arrange the plum halves in rows across the dough and sprinkle with the crumble.

Bake for 30–35 minutes or until golden. Let it cool for 5–10 minutes before cutting and enjoying warm or at room temperature.

Travel advice
Wrap with a tea towel and place in a flat basket or tray, or cut into slices and pile into a tin. If at all warm, don't cover with an airtight lid or it might go soggy.

Note
It's ideal but not necessary to use pastry flour for this recipe, as it has a slightly higher protein content than plain (all-purpose) flour, but if you can't find it then plain (all-purpose) flour will work just as well.

What Can I Bring?

Apricot and almond granola jars

When it's too hot to bake, but you'd like to contribute something sweet to morning tea, brunch or breakfast gatherings, these little jars of granola, yoghurt and fruit are a great option. And yes, you could definitely use a nice store-bought granola, but home-made does take everything up a notch. I make granola most weeks, and in summer, when stone fruit is plentiful and affordable, I love using a purée of apricots or peaches in place of other sweeteners. The resulting flavour is just delicious.

Prep time 30 mins
Cook time 1 hour 20 mins
Serves 4

Apricot granola
12 apricots (approx. 500 g/
  1 lb 2 oz), halved and stones
  removed
½ cup (175 g) honey (depending
  on how sweet your fruit is)
Juice of 1 lemon
1 tsp vanilla paste
4 cups (400 g) rolled oats
2 cups (35 g) puffed quinoa
  or millet
1 cup (160 g) whole almonds,
  roughly chopped

To assemble
4 apricots, halved, stones
  removed, thinly sliced
250 g (9 oz) strawberries,
  hulled and quartered
Juice of 1 lemon
1 Tbsp sugar
2 cups (520 g) Greek-style
  yoghurt

Preheat the oven to 160°C (315°F).

To make your purée for the granola, place the apricots, half of the honey, lemon juice, vanilla and 2 tablespoons water in a large saucepan over low heat. Cook, stirring often, for about 10 minutes, or until the fruit has softened and completely collapsed. Transfer to a blender and purée until smooth.

Spread the mixture in a large roasting tin and bake for 30 minutes, stirring about halfway through so that nothing sticks to the bottom and burns. This should yield about 3 cups (750 ml) purée.

Lower the temperature of the oven to 150°C (300°F). Place the oats, quinoa and almonds in a large bowl and tip in 2 cups (500 ml) of the purée and the remaining honey. Toss to combine (careful if the purée is still hot), then pull out another roasting tin and divide the mixture between the two. Return to the oven for about 40 minutes, taking each tray out every 15 minutes or so to toss the mixture around so that nothing catches and burns.

Once the granola is golden brown, turn the oven off and leave the granola inside to cool.

When you're almost ready to assemble your granola jars, combine the sliced apricots, strawberries, lemon juice and sugar in a small bowl and set aside to macerate for 10 minutes. The sugar and lemon juice should draw moisture from the fruit and create a lovely syrupy sauce.

Grab four 1-cup (250-ml) capacity jars and start with a layer of yoghurt, then a little of the remaining apricot purée, a little granola, a little fruit and then repeat so you have a few layers per jar. Seal and keep in the fridge till serving. Make up to 6 hours in advance – any earlier than that and the granola might lose its crunch.

Travel advice
Keep chilled right up until serving. If that's going to be half a day or more from assembly time, pack up all the elements separately and assemble on site (to avoid the granola going soft).

Fabulous focaccia

This is perhaps the thing I make the most, with the most success and the most joy. A big, golden slab of crunchy, salty focaccia cut into warm little cubes, or big squares, is always well received, and it's the perfect canvas for all kinds of seasonal toppings. But where it shines the most is at a drinks party – those gatherings where you want to contribute something substantial to eat and something easy to transport and share. Especially when in a paddock at sunset! For the occasion pictured, I made a couple of different focaccias and packed them in a basket with a jar of pickles (see page 188), a few chunks of cheese (a cheddar and a soft white) and a jar of spiced nuts. This became a simple but properly tasty spread that we grazed on while gazing at the view from our farm that I love most of all.

Overnight focaccia

Prep time 45 mins, plus proving
Cook time 30 mins
Makes two 20 × 30 cm
  (8 × 12 inch) focaccias

1 kg (2 lb 4 oz) high-protein
  white baker's flour
2 tsp dry yeast
1 tsp honey
20 g (¾ oz) salt
Olive oil, for drizzling

This recipe's long, cold fermentation builds a beautifully chewy texture and sour flavour that I love. And while the whole process does take up to a day, the actual 'hands-on' time is under an hour. Feel free to play around with different toppings, shapes and sizes. This dough is also great for pizzas, or you could make a bunch of mini focaccias, which are ideal for lunch boxes.

Step 1 (Let's say we're starting at 6pm)

Combine the flour, yeast, 800 ml (28 fl oz) room-temperature water and the honey in a large bowl and, using your hands, work the mixture until you have a sticky, shaggy dough. Cover with a tea towel and leave for 30 minutes.

Step 2 (6.30pm)

Add the salt and another 40 ml (1¼ fl oz) water and mix with your hands again. Cover and leave for another 30 minutes.

Step 3 (7–9pm)

Now we will do four 'stretch and folds' every half an hour for the next 2 hours. So, for the first one, start with damp hands and scoop about one-quarter of the dough up from one side, stretch it up and fold over the rest. Spin the bowl a quarter turn, scoop and stretch, and repeat until you've done four folds. Cover the bowl again and leave for another half an hour. Repeat this process three more times every half an hour.

Step 4 (9pm)

Now we're ready for the bulk fermentation stage, which means we will put the dough in the fridge overnight or for up to 24 hours to rise slowly.

Step 5 (7am)

I would like my focaccia for lunch, so we'll take the dough out of the fridge in the morning, turn it out onto a benchtop and divide it into two. Shape each piece into a flat disc, cover with a tea towel and leave at room temperature for another 30 minutes.

Step 6 (7.30am)

Drizzle a little olive oil into two roasting tins and, using your hands, rub it all over the base of the tins. Gently transfer a disc of dough into each tin and, even gentler still, begin pressing and pushing it to fit. It won't give much straight away, but that's why we'll leave the dough now to relax for a while.

Step 7 (11.30am)

Preheat the oven to 200°C (400°F). It's been 4 hours since we placed the dough into the tins, but you could halve this time if it's hot where you are. It's not an exact science at this stage! Nevertheless, we're finally close to cooking.

Now is the time to press in whatever toppings you're going with (see opposite for some ideas). I read once that you might approach pressing into focaccia dough like you're playing the piano softly – gentle pressing rather than prodding. And because the dough will rise as it bakes, as we want it to, you want to push your toppings quite deep into the dough, or they might pop up and burn as they cook.

Drizzle with a little more olive oil and perhaps sprinkle with sea salt, depending on whatever else you've added on top. Cook your focaccia for 30 minutes, or until puffed and deeply golden.

Step 8 (12pm onwards)

Yum! You're done.

Variations

CONFIT GARLIC AND ROSEMARY FOCACCIA

For the confit, take 1 garlic head and carefully peel each clove. Pop these in a small saucepan and cover with 1½ cups (375 ml) olive oil. Place over the lowest heat possible and infuse for 30 minutes or so. You want the garlic cloves to have turned a light golden colour but not burned.

Grab a jar and pop in a rosemary sprig, then pour in the garlic cloves and oil. Seal and store in the fridge.

For the focaccia, follow the recipe opposite, but right before you are ready to bake, dot the top of your lovely bubbly dough with about 10 confit garlic cloves and drizzle with the olive oil. Top with a few sprigs of rosemary and bake until golden.

CARAMELISED ONION FOCACCIA

Heat 20 g (¾ oz) butter and 2 tablespoons olive oil in a deep-sided frying pan, then add 4 thinly sliced brown onions. Cook over low heat for about 30 minutes until deeply caramelised and soft. Leave to cool, then spread across your focaccia. Press in and drizzle with extra olive oil and sea salt right before baking.

APPLE, CHEDDAR AND THYME FOCACCIA

Place 3 thinly sliced red apples in a large bowl. Sprinkle with 1½ cups (150 g) grated cheddar and 3 tablespoons thyme leaves. Drizzle in about 3 tablespoons olive oil and 1 teaspoon sea salt and gently toss to combine. Press this mixture into the top of your focaccia right before it goes into the oven.

FIG AND HAZELNUT FOCACCIA

When your focaccia is ready to go in the oven, gently press in 8 quartered figs and 1 cup (120 g) roughly chopped roasted hazelnuts. Drizzle with a little extra olive oil and sprinkle with sea salt, then bake.

Travel advice

Once baked and cooled, these focaccias travel well in an airtight container. They can be warmed in the oven or sliced and toasted when you arrive.

The whole shebang

Sometimes you don't just want to take a plate, you want to take the whole shebang – an entire meal that cheers, comforts and delights. And this one does all three. It comes a little from me, but mostly from Mudgee-based winemaker Jean-François Esnault, who calls his chicken, ratatouille and crêpe menu 'a love poem to my wife' (baker extraordinaire Rebecca Sutton). These two entertain with such style – always good wine and bread (of course), and a table outside crammed with friends.

To Jean-François's menu I have added a simple pork terrine, which is an easy and excellent starter (with good bread, pickles, butter and chilled rosé). It's also handy to take to someone who needs feeding over a few days.

Simple pork terrine

A simple 'cut and come again' terrine like this is not only a great thing to make and take to a party or gathering, but it's also super handy to have in the fridge for lunches. Especially during summer when everyone is home and seems to be ducking in and out of the house to eat at odd hours between farm jobs (or whatever the kids might be doing). A thick slice of this terrine between two pieces of bread with tomato relish and some greens makes a terrific and very filling sandwich.

Prep time 20 mins, plus chilling
Cook time 1 hour 40 mins
Serves 8–10

1 brown onion, finely diced
2 Tbsp olive oil
10 rashers streaky bacon
500 g (1 lb 2 oz) pork shoulder, finely diced (your butcher should be able to do this, or cut and then dice in a food processor) or 500 g (1 lb 2 oz) minced (ground) pork
6 good-quality pork and fennel sausages
1 small handful sage leaves, finely chopped
2 garlic cloves, finely chopped
½ tsp sea salt
1 tsp freshly ground nutmeg
½ tsp allspice
1 tsp freshly ground pepper
1 egg
½ cup (75 g) dried cranberries
1 cup (115 g) walnut halves, toasted and roughly chopped
Cornichons, relish and crusty bread, to serve

Place the onion in a frying pan with the olive oil and cook over medium heat for about 10 minutes, or until completely soft and translucent. Spread the onion out on a tray to cool completely.

Preheat the oven to 160°C (315°F) and line a loaf tin with the bacon, placing three strips lengthways along the bottom of the tin and the rest crossways. Allow the ends to hang over the sides.

Place the diced pork shoulder or minced pork in a large bowl, then squeeze the sausage meat from its casings and add that, too. Next, add the sage, garlic, salt, nutmeg, allspice, pepper, egg, cranberries and walnuts. Mix everything with your hands then transfer to the loaf tin, pressing down quite firmly.

Fold the bacon over the top to make a sort of lid and wrap tightly in foil. Line a roasting tin with a tea towel then place the terrine in the middle (this will stop the tin from moving around). Place the roasting tin on the middle rack of your oven and carefully pour enough hot water into the tin to reach halfway up the terrine.

Cook for 1½ hours then remove and leave to cool for about 15 minutes in the water bath. Weigh down the top with a few tins of tomatoes or such and refrigerate overnight or for at least 6 hours. Serve with cornichons, relish and crusty bread.

Travel advice
Try not to serve this terrine fridge-cold but give it about 10 minutes at room temperature before slicing and sharing around. Keep thoroughly chilled right up until this point.

Really, really good roast chicken with orange and bay

I know. It might seem odd at first to suggest a roast chicken as a portable dish, but why not? Don't we all love picking up a hot rotisserie chicken on the way to a picnic or for a quick meal? Jean-François's recipe is the same only so much better (and cheaper). Here, the bird's cavity is stuffed with orange, lemon and bay leaves, and these flavours infuse the chicken as it cooks.

Prep time 15 mins
Cook time 1 hour
Serves 6

1 whole chicken (about 1.6 kg/
3 lb 8 oz) (the best you can get
  your hands on)
2 oranges
2 lemons
2 Tbsp extra virgin olive oil,
  plus extra for drizzling
A small bouquet of garden herbs
  (thyme, rosemary, sage), finely
  chopped
3 bay leaves
Buttered boiled potatoes,
  to serve
Ratatouille (page 105), to serve

Preheat the oven to 200°C (400°F) and line a roasting tin with baking paper. Drizzle with a little olive oil and place the chicken on top.

Combine the zest and juice of one each of the lemons and oranges and place in a bowl. Add the olive oil, bouquet of herbs and a good amount of salt and freshly ground pepper.

Cut the other orange and lemon into quarters and stuff these inside the chicken with the bay leaves. Pour the juice and olive oil mixture over the chicken and place in the oven for 1 hour, or until the skin has turned crispy and golden. Every 20 minutes or so, baste the chicken with the pan juices and turn the tray around in the oven to ensure everything cooks evenly.

Once cooked, remove from the oven and cover the tray with foil. One way to check if your chicken is cooked through is to prod the thickest part of the meat and if the juices run clear it is cooked. If you have a digital meat thermometer, the temperature should be 165°C (330°F). Let the chicken rest for at least 20 minutes before carving and serving with the buttered potatoes and ratatouille.

Travel advice
If the intention is to serve your chicken cold, then please allow it to chill right down before leaving the house, and maybe make it the day before. Transport in an insulated ice box or cooler. If hot, time things so the chook is coming out of the oven right before you head off, wrap it tightly in foil and place in a snug airtight container, wrap that in a towel and it should stay warm for an hour.

Ratatouille

On sharing this recipe, Jean-François told me that ratatouille is all about vegetables coming together in perfect harmony. How lovely is that? Let's all be like ratatouille. And what a delicious way to celebrate summer's harvest. Make this dish well ahead if you prefer, and serve at room temperature or reheat right before lunch. I highly recommend doubling this recipe - tasty leftovers for days!

Prep time 15 mins
Cook time 50 mins
Serves 4-6 people

100 ml (3½ fl oz) olive oil
1 eggplant (aubergine), destemmed, cut into quarters, then sliced (not too thin)
2 zucchini (courgettes), halved and sliced into 1-2 cm (½-¾ inch) pieces
1 red capsicum (pepper), halved, seeded and cut into 2-3 cm (¾-1¼ inch) dice
1 brown onion, thinly sliced
½ fennel bulb, halved and thinly sliced
1 big handful cherry tomatoes or cocktail tomatoes
800 g (1 lb 12 oz) tin whole peeled Italian tomatoes
1 tsp smoked paprika
A pinch of chilli powder

Heat a couple of tablespoons of the olive oil in a large frying pan. Add the eggplant and sauté with a good sprinkle of salt and pepper. Add a little more olive oil as you go, as eggplant can get quite 'thirsty'. Cook for about 10 minutes, or until soft, then transfer to a bowl.

Add a little more oil to the frying pan then add the zucchini and sauté with a pinch of salt for 5-10 minutes or until soft. Transfer to the bowl with the eggplant.

Again, add a little more oil to your pan, and now add the capsicum, onion and fennel. These three can be sautéed together as they have roughly the same cooking times – about 15 minutes. Again, season with salt and pepper as you go.

Tip in the cherry tomatoes and give them 'a quick trip in the pan' just to soften them gently. A little more olive oil, salt and pepper, of course.

Combine all the sautéed vegetables and the tinned tomatoes in the pan over low heat. Add the spices and check the flavour – a good amount of paprika and enough chilli to just taste it is what we're looking for. Stir gently until you can sense 'harmony between all the vegetables' (side note: I love how Jean-François describes cooking this dish). The crushed tomatoes will take on a different colour in this process, the cherry tomatoes will have softened and fallen apart, and all the vegetables will be cooked, but there should still be a little crunch in the capsicum and fennel.

Serve at room temperature. Ratatouille is also beautiful reheated the next day and served at breakfast with an egg on top.

Travel advice
Another super easy, forgiving dish. I'd cook this the day before or morning of and then transport in an airtight container before serving at room temperature.

Sugar crêpes

Making beautiful thin crêpes like these isn't hard, but it takes practice to pour and flip them with French flair à la Jean-François. And, as he says, once you master this basic recipe you can take them in any direction you like, sweet or savoury. 'I thought when I met Rebecca,' he tells me from his position at the stove, two pans going at once, 'If I am going to woo that woman, I'll need more than just my pretty face. I'll have to bring out the crêpe pan.'

Prep time 10 mins
Cook time 40 mins
Makes approx. 20

2 cups (500 ml) full-cream milk
4 eggs
1⅔ cups (250 g) plain
   (all-purpose) flour
100 g (3½ oz) salted butter,
   cubed, plus extra melted butter
   for brushing
200 g (7 oz) raw sugar

Combine the milk, 2 cups (500 ml) water, the eggs and flour in a jug and whisk until you have a smooth batter. Set aside for at least 30 minutes before cooking, or place in the fridge for up to 12 hours.

Brush a 20 cm (8 inch) frying pan (ideally a crêpe pan but the flattest pan you have will do) with a little melted butter and ladle about ½ cup (125 ml) batter into the hot pan while tilting it with the other hand to ensure the pan's surface is well covered. The amount of batter you use per crêpe will depend on the size of your pan, so adjust accordingly.

Cook for about 1 minute, then gently loosen the sides of the crêpe with a spatula. Once it feels cooked enough, slide the whole spatula under the crêpe and flip. Lift one side of the crêpe and place a cube of butter underneath, sprinkle about 1 teaspoon raw sugar on top, then place the crêpe back down and cook for another minute. The butter and sugar will caramelise as they cook. Continue with the remaining butter, batter and sugar. Keep your cooked crêpes warm under a tent of foil or in a very low oven.

Travel advice

You can cook the crêpes up to a day in advance. Wrap them in paper towel and transport in an airtight container. Enjoy cold, or reheat them in a frying pan with a little butter and a sprinkle of sugar.

More crêpe ideas from Jean-François

Honey and rosemary butter Finely chop about 1 tablespoon fresh rosemary leaves and mix with 100 g (3½ oz) soft salted butter. Spread this on top of your crêpes as they are hot out of the pan and drizzle with a little honey.

Ham and cheese Grate your favourite cheese on one half of the crêpe while it is still in the pan, add a slice or two of good ham then flip the other half of the crêpe on top. Transfer to a plate and enjoy!

Smoked salmon, cheese and rocket Spread cream cheese on one half of the crêpe in the pan, top with a few slices of smoked salmon and flip the other half of the crêpe on top. Transfer to a plate, tuck in some rocket (arugula) and add a squeeze of lemon.

Nothing (but something)

When it's Christmas (or any) time, and your lovely host says 'please don't bring a thing' but you still want to bring a little thank-you gift, may I suggest a jar of spiced biscuits? Or, better yet, a jar of biscuits with a selection of chocolates thrown in too.

There's a beautiful German Christmas tradition of baking biscuits throughout Advent to have on hand as a 'Bunter Teller': a plate of assorted biscuits to share with visitors who drop in for coffee over the festive period.

Each plate is assembled with a particular recipient in mind, with thought given to what biscuits they love best.

I've since adopted the practice and love putting together colourful, delicious plates (or jars) to take to friends, as a treat for the kids and/ or to share in place of dessert. And it's not just a Christmas thing. A thoughtful little selection of treats will always surprise and delight, year round. My take on Bunter Teller always seems to include a spiced biscuit or two and some chocolates.

Things to bring when you're asked not to bring anything

- **A bunch of herbs or flowers** in a jar of water
- **A few packets of seeds** (extra points if you've dried and saved them from your own garden)
- **A favourite book** that you think your friend might like, too
- **A jar of apricot and almond granola** (see page 89)
- **A mixed box of biscuits**, such as Dark chocolate tahini biscuits (page 141), Jammy macaroons (page 142), Fruity nutty oat biscuits (page 142), Orange and rhubarb melting moments (page 140)
- **A jar of Toum (Garlic dip)** (page 170)
- **A crostata** (see page 155)
- **A jar of dukkah** (see page 113)
- **A loaf cake** (see pages 209–10)
- **A jar of Irish coffee mix** (page 205)
- **A container of frozen sausage rolls** (see page 28)
- **A jar of chocolate Crinkle biscuits** (page 69)
- **A box of Strawberry jam crumble slice** (page 55)
- **A box of Rocky road** (page 132)
- **A jar of White chocolate-dipped pretzels** (page 132)
- **A bag of fresh coffee beans**
- **A pot plant**
- **A cutting from your garden**
- **Fresh eggs** tied in a cute tea towel
- **Wine** (this is always a good idea!)
- **A jar of jam** and a nice loaf of bread
- **A handwritten recipe**

A progressive dinner

How are progressive meals not more of a thing? I'm a recent convert to the idea of breaking up meals into a number of menu 'stops' at different locations. Firstly, because you get to talk to everyone properly. Secondly, it takes the pressure off just one person to cook and host. And thirdly, it's so fun.

My friend Em and I share a birthday, the 30th December. It's a funny time because everyone's still coming down from Christmas and saving up for New Year's Eve celebrations, but we often try to do something together, and last year was a doozy. We organised a progressive dinner through our farm with food by me and wines matched by Em. It's helpful that she and her family have a winery here in Orange (Printhie Wines) – they make a truly beautiful range.

I can't recommend doing something like this enough. There was a bit of admin and quite a lot of prep involved but it was so worth it. And while I cooked all seven stops for this event (so I could shoot it and share with you!), I will definitely farm out all but one or two next time.

We started our day at 4pm and meandered along a 4 kilometre (2½ mile) track through the farm and finished well into the early hours of the next day. If you're in a more urban area, why not get together with a few neighbourhood friends and walk between houses? Or you could line up a couple of families within a short drive of each other.

Here's the menu we enjoyed. I so hope you try one, two or all of these lovely dishes, ideally each in a different location!

MENU

Feast.

Elderflower gin cocktail

Ed's vibrant, zingy cocktail was the perfect way to kick off our progressive dinner party.

Combine 1½ cups (325 ml) gin, 2 cups (500 ml) elderflower cordial, 2 bottles sparkling wine, 3 cups (750 ml) soda water and 2 sliced limes in a large jug or bowl with plenty of ice. Mix well and serve.

Travel advice
Keep everything chilled in an insulated cooler and mix up just before serving in a big jug with lots of ice.

Freshly shucked oysters

When you have beautiful fresh oysters I don't think you need to do much except squeeze a little lemon juice over them and enjoy au natural.

Travel advice
If your oysters are unshucked, they should travel in an insulated ice box or cooler, ideally wrapped in a damp tea towel. Consume as soon as they're opened and, ideally, serve on a bed of ice to keep really cold.

Prosciutto-wrapped peaches with hazelnut dukkah and balsamic glaze

A super simple, summery starter, this one is that perfect marriage of sweet, salty and crunchy. It's beautiful with perfectly ripe peaches, melon or figs.

Prep time 25 mins
Cook time 10 mins
Serves 6–8

8 slices prosciutto
4 ripe yellow slipstone peaches, stones removed, quartered
250 g (9 oz) mozzarella, sliced quite thinly

Hazelnut dukkah
¼ cup (40 g) sesame seeds
1 tsp coriander seeds
1 tsp cumin seeds
1 tsp sea salt
½ cup (75 g) toasted hazelnuts
½ tsp dried chilli flakes, or to taste

Thyme balsamic vinegar glaze
150 ml (5 fl oz) balsamic vinegar
2 Tbsp caster (superfine) sugar
2 thyme sprigs

Let's start with the dukkah. Place the sesame seeds in a dry frying pan over medium heat and toast until pale golden. Add the coriander and cumin seeds and toast for a couple more minutes until aromatic. Tip into a mortar and pestle or food processor, add the salt and hazelnuts, and pound or blitz to a rough crumb. Add the chilli, mix well and store in a jar or airtight container for up to 2 weeks.

For the glaze, bring all the ingredients to the boil in a small saucepan. Reduce the heat to low and simmer until the mixture thickens and reduces by half, about 5 minutes. Transfer to a jar and keep in the fridge. It should thicken up as it cools.

Separate the prosciutto slices and cut in half lengthways. Take one piece of prosciutto, lay a peach quarter on top, add a slice of mozzarella and a good sprinkle of the dukkah. Wrap the prosciutto tightly and arrange on a nice platter. Repeat with the remaining ingredients, then keep refrigerated or in an insulated ice box or cooler until needed.

Just before serving, sprinkle with a little more dukkah and drizzle with the glaze.

Travel advice
Do everything except drizzle with the glaze and sprinkle with the dukkah up to a day in advance.

Spiced gazpacho with chilli cheddar shortbreads

Like all simple recipes, this one relies on the best ingredients to really shine. Use the best tomatoes (ripe and at room temperature) and olive oil (fruity and fresh) you can get your hands on. I added a little vodka to each small cup (just enough to give a tiny punch), but you can leave it out if you prefer. The buttery, spicy shortbreads are the perfect companion to our little shots of cold soup.

Prep time 10 mins, plus chilling
Cook time 20–25 mins
Serves 8–10 as a starter

500 g (1 lb 2 oz) ripe tomatoes
1 tsp sea salt
1 tsp freshly ground black pepper
Juice of 1 lemon
¼ tsp smoked paprika
¼ tsp freshly grated horseradish, or horseradish cream
¼ cup (60 ml) extra virgin olive oil
Vodka (optional), to taste

Chilli cheddar shortbreads
1⅓ cups (200 g) plain (all-purpose) flour
2 tsp mustard powder
2 tsp dried chilli flakes
1 tsp freshly ground black pepper
1 tsp sea salt
⅔ cup (160 g) unsalted butter, chilled and cubed
2½ cups (250 g) coarsely grated cheddar

To make the shortbreads, combine all the ingredients in a food processor and blitz until the mixture just comes together. Turn out onto a benchtop and roll into a sausage, then cut into four even lengths, cover and refrigerate for least an hour.

Preheat the oven to 180°C (350°F) and line a couple of baking trays with baking paper.

Cut two of the chilled dough pieces into 1 cm (½ inch) rounds and arrange on the trays. Bake for 10–12 minutes or until pale golden, then repeat with the remaining dough. Leave all the biscuits to cool completely on wire racks. (Store in an airtight container for up to 2 weeks.)

For the gazpacho, chop the tomatoes, place in a blender with the salt, pepper, lemon juice, paprika and horseradish and then blitz (work in batches if necessary, but bring it back together for the next step).

Reduce the blender speed to medium and add the olive oil in a thin stream so it emulsifies as you go. Check the flavour, adjusting the seasoning and acidity to taste.

Transfer to the fridge to chill for at least 4 hours; you want it to be icy cold. The flavour can dull a little once chilled, so you might need to add another squeeze of lemon or pinch of salt.

Serve in small glasses with a splash of vodka to taste, if using, and some chilli cheddar shortbreads for dipping.

Travel advice
Pour the completely chilled soup into a thermos (which has been cooled down with iced water first). Add a few ice cubes and seal tightly.

Focaccia, salami and cheese

For this stop, I made a few big slabs of focaccia (see pages 94-5), bought some good salami and cheese and made up a few platters. By this stage in our walk, everyone was ready for some carbs and substantial snacks!

Travel advice
Wrap the focaccia in a clean tea towel and slice on arrival. If it's a hot day, keep the salami chilled until ready to serve. Bring the cheese to room temperature, if possible.

Tuna ceviche with coconut and lime

Ceviche is an umbrella term for infinite ways you can 'cook' raw fish with citrus juice (aka acid). On a hot summer evening when you crave something with zing, tang and crunch for a starter or main, it's wonderful. Word on the street (or paddock) was that this took out the popular 'vote' for our progressive dinner and it was an easy win; you just cut everything up quite small and pack it into a container then keep chilled. Pack and chill the dressing, too. Then, 15 minutes or so before serving, combine the two and spoon into little pita cups.

Prep time 20 mins, plus
  marinating
Cook time NIL
Serves 8–10 as a starter

Coconut dressing
½ cup (125 ml) coconut milk
Juice of 4 limes, zest of 2 limes
1 tsp brown sugar
1 bunch coriander (cilantro),
  stalks finely chopped, leaves
  kept aside
1 long red chilli, halved, seeded
  and finely chopped
2 Tbsp finely grated fresh ginger

To assemble
600 g (1 lb 5 oz) sashimi-grade
  tuna, cut into 1–2 cm (½–
  ¾ inch) dice (you might need
  to order this ahead from your
  seafood shop or supermarket)
2 cucumbers, seeded and finely
  chopped
2 avocados, stones removed,
  diced
250 g (9 oz) cherry tomatoes,
  quartered

To serve
20–30 pita cups (see right)
1 cup (100 g) fried shallots

Start with the dressing. Mix the coconut milk, lime zest and juice, the brown sugar, 2 tablespoons of the chopped coriander stalks, the chilli and ginger in a jar, seal and shake well. Check the flavour. If you think it needs more lime or a tiny bit of sugar to round things out, then adjust and pop in the fridge till needed.

Combine the tuna, cucumber, avocado, tomato and a handful of the coriander leaves in a bowl or container.

Pour the coconut mixture over the fish mixture and toss well. Set aside at room temperature for about 15 minutes, in which time the acidity in the lime juice should 'cook' the fish just until its exterior firms up but not all the way through.

Spoon into the pita cups, top with a sprinkle of the fried shallots and pass around.

Travel advice
Don't mix the coconut dressing with the fish mixture until 15 minutes before serving. Any sooner than that and the acidity can cause the fish to toughen up a bit. Keep the fish mixture and dressing nice and cold. One idea is to serve this on a bed of ice, see page 66.

Pita cups
1. Preheat the oven to 180°C (350°F).
2. Use a glass or small round cookie cutter to cut out rounds of pita bread to fit a mini muffin tin (I used a scalloped-edge cutter that fit our tin perfectly). If your pita bread feels a bit dry and likely to tear, then pop it in the microwave for 15 seconds or so to soften up, then gently press into the muffin tin.
3. Bake for 10–15 minutes or until pale golden brown.
4. Store in an airtight container for about a week. You can always skip the 'cup' step here and just cut the pita bread into triangles if that's easier.

Travel advice
Make sure your pita cups have fully cooled before transporting in an airtight container.

Slow-cooked beef

I don't know of an easier, more crowd-pleasing thing to make for a big group than slow-cooked beef. You can make it the day before then just slice and serve. It was perfect for our progressive dinner as we had it sitting in a cooler for the afternoon and it was ready for us to carve up on arrival.

Prep time 5 mins
Cook time 1 hour 10 mins
Serves 6–8

1.5 kg (3 lb 5 oz) beef fillet, at room temperature
¼ cup (60 ml) olive oil
¼ cup (60 ml) white wine
Slow-cooked capsicums with horseradish and balsamic (page 81), to serve
Quick pickled beetroot with sorrel mayonnaise (see right), to serve

Preheat the oven to 120°C (235°F).
  Rub the beef well with the oil and some salt and pepper and brown well in a skillet over high heat. Transfer to a roasting tin and cook in the oven, uncovered, for 1 hour. This should yield a super tender result.
  Transfer to a board and cover with a tent of foil to cool. Tip the pan juices into a small saucepan, add the wine and bring to the boil, then reduce by half.
  If serving the beef warm, slice now and serve on a bed of the warm capsicums with the reduced pan juices spooned over the top. If serving cold, wrap tightly in plastic wrap and keep in the fridge until needed. When serving cold, I like to slice it thinly and serve on the warm capsicums. This is what we did for our dinner, and I kept the capsicums warm in an insulated food bowl. Serve the pickled beetroot and sorrel mayonnaise on the side.

Travel advice
Transport in an insulated ice box or cooler. Remove 20–30 minutes before serving to allow the meat to come up to temperature.

Quick pickled beetroot with sorrel mayonnaise

Sorrel packs a serious citrus punch. Here it imparts a beautiful green colour and lots of tang.

Prep time 30 mins, plus pickling
Cook time 5 mins
Serves 6–8 / Makes 1 cup (235 g) mayonnaise

1 Tbsp fennel seeds
2 cups (500 ml) apple cider vinegar
3 thyme sprigs
2 Tbsp sugar
4–6 beetroot (beets), peeled

Sorrel mayonnaise
2 egg yolks
1 Tbsp dijon mustard
½ tsp sea salt
½ cup (125 ml) vegetable oil
½ cup (125 ml) olive oil
1 handful sorrel leaves, very finely chopped

Dry-toast the fennel seeds in a small saucepan over medium–high heat for a few minutes or until fragrant. Pour in the vinegar and 1 cup (250 ml) water. Whisk in the thyme and sugar, then bring to the boil. Remove from the heat and whisk again to dissolve the sugar, then leave to cool for 10 minutes.
  Slice the beetroot as thinly as you can (I use a mandolin) and place in a bowl. Pour in the vinegar mixture, toss well, then cover and refrigerate to pickle for at least 4 hours but up to 3 days.
  To make the sorrel mayonnaise, place the yolks, mustard and salt in a bowl and whisk to combine.
  Combine the oils in a jug and gradually add to the yolk mixture in a steady stream, whisking constantly until the mixture emulsifies into a thick mayonnaise (it will thicken further on refrigeration). Fold in the sorrel, transfer to a jar and keep in the fridge for 2–3 days. Serve alongside the beetroot for dolloping on top.

Travel advice
Transport both in airtight containers in an insulated ice box or cooler and serve chilled.

From left: Cucumber salad with soy-roasted seeds and miso dressing (page 120); Slow-cooked beef; Quick pickled beetroot with sorrel mayonnaise; Burghul pilaf with roasted zucchini (page 120)

Burghul pilaf with roasted zucchini

This dish is easy to pull together and makes the perfect bed for our tender roast beef. It will happily sit around for ages and is great for al fresco dinners. You could add more roasted vegetables and some nuts for crunch and make it a main meal as well.

Prep time 10 mins
Cook time 1 hour
Serves 6–8 as a side dish

¼ cup (60 ml) olive oil
2 garlic cloves, finely chopped
Zest and juice of 2 lemons
1 tsp smoked paprika
1 tsp ground cumin
250 g (9 oz) burghul
4 zucchini (courgettes), trimmed
  and sliced into 2 cm (¾ inch) rounds

Heat half the olive oil in a large ovenproof dish with a well-fitting lid over medium heat. Add the garlic, lemon zest, paprika and cumin and cook for 2 minutes, stirring as you go. Add the burghul and cook, stirring for a couple of minutes to coat in the spiced oil.

Preheat the oven to 180°C (350°F).

Add 2 cups (500 ml) water to the burghul, bring to the boil, then cover and reduce the heat to low. Cook for 20 minutes then remove from the heat. Remove the lid, place a tea towel on top of the dish, then replace the lid and set aside until ready to serve. This helps keep the heat in while absorbing any extra moisture.

Meanwhile, place the zucchini on a baking tray, drizzle with the remaining oil, season well with salt and pepper and roast for 40 minutes, or until it is golden and beginning to caramelise.

To serve, pile the burghul on a platter and top with the roasted zucchini. Squeeze over the lemon juice to taste.

Travel advice
This dish is happy to sit at room temperature for up to 2 hours. Transport in a sealed container.

• *Pictured page 119*

Cucumber salad with soy-roasted seeds and miso dressing

With plenty of crunch and loads of flavour, this salad brings a lot to the table!

Prep time 20 mins, plus chilling
Cook time 15 mins
Serves 6–8

6 Lebanese (short) cucumbers
1 tsp sea salt
1 cup (155 g) pepitas (pumpkin seeds)
½ cup (75 g) sesame seeds
3 Tbsp soy sauce
½ tsp chilli flakes (optional)
3 spring onions (scallions), finely chopped

Tahini dressing
1 Tbsp tahini
Juice of 3 limes
1 Tbsp soy sauce
1 Tbsp white miso paste
1 tsp honey
3 cm (1¼ inch) piece ginger, peeled and finely grated
1 garlic clove, finely grated

Cut the cucumbers in half lengthways, then into thick diagonal slices. Place in a bowl, add the salt and toss well. Cover and chill for at least 3 hours, then tip into a colander and leave to drain.

Preheat the oven to 180°C (350°F). Place all the seeds in a roasting tin and add the soy sauce and chilli flakes. Toss well, then toast for 10 minutes. Toss again, then return to the oven for another 5 minutes if needed to crisp up. Leave to cool, then transfer to a container or jar. (Keep leftovers for up to 2 weeks.)

For the dressing, add everything to a big jar and shake to combine. Check and adjust the flavour.

Transfer the cucumber to a platter, drizzle with the dressing and top with the spring onion and seeds.

Travel advice
Pack the seed mixture, salad and dressing separately. Keep the two latter elements cool until assembling.

• *Pictured page 119*

Dessert 'pick and mix'

After such a big meal (and walk), and on such a warm evening, I didn't think we'd feel like a heavy pudding, so instead I put together three big tins of treats to share around. I love a 'pick and mix' dessert like this: chocolate, fruit, sweets, nougat - whatever you fancy. There's no washing up and people can graze and take what they feel like.

Tips for running a progressive dinner or lunch

If you're feeling inspired to organise your own progressive lunch or dinner, here are some tips to help it run smoothly:

- Start with the 'route' and then decide how many stops and where. You could go from house to house in your street, neighbourhood or building, or perhaps pick a park or beach. (Everyone would have to carry their own meal but that's totally doable!)
- Allocate everyone a stop. Or, if you're a big group, put two people together per stop, one to look after food and one drinks.
- If you like, choose an overall theme for everyone: a style of cuisine (French, Moroccan, Japanese, your favourite), an era (the seventies) or a cookbook. This helps to make the menu more cohesive.
- If doing this in summer and outside, buy more ice than you think you'll need. Borrow insulated coolers so that each 'stop' has a cooler full of ice ready to load up.
- Charge your solar lights at least two days out!

Autumn.

Camping trips, farm picnics, big family feasts and baking sessions to fill all the biscuit jars… autumn is my favourite season for cooking and gathering. I especially love the cooler days, beautiful produce and lack of flies!

Salads of substance

The majority of our entertaining happens outside, up on the ridge paddock of our farm near Orange, New South Wales. This is mostly because the view there is my favourite in the world, unfolding west for miles in a patchwork of paddocks, scrub, forest and the odd olive grove. But also, because we have a small house and it gets crowded and hectic quite quickly.

The recipes on the following pages are pretty much the blueprint for these outings: a few hearty salads, some chops and perhaps chicken cooked over the fire, then a tin or two of biscuits or cake. Often, friends bring the latter and they are always special days. This style of eating is easier than you think... all you need is to set the date, delegate parts of the meal, pick a spot (park, garden, beach, wherever), and have yourself a wonderful afternoon. And why don't we do it more often? Let's steal time back and have a picnic this weekend.

Super herby potato salad

Even though it's autumnal in feel, this salad is great for the summer, too, as it doesn't contain any dairy or mayonnaise that will spoil if left out at room temperature, and all that lemon and the herbs bring comfort plus zing and lightness. I would take this potato salad over its mayonnaise-heavy counterpart any day.

Prep time 15 mins
Cook time 15 mins
Serves 6–8

1 kg (2 lb 4 oz) baby potatoes, halved or quartered if large
2 Tbsp salt
3 Tbsp tarragon leaves
1 good handful dill
1 good handful parsley leaves
1 good handful mint leaves
2 Tbsp dijon mustard
½ cup (125 ml) extra virgin olive oil
¼ cup (60 ml) white wine vinegar
½ tsp honey
3 crisp green apples, cored and finely sliced (into matchsticks is great)

Place the potatoes and salt in a large pot and cover with water. Bring to a simmer over medium–high heat and cook until the potatoes are tender, about 15 minutes. Drain and leave until still warm but cool enough to handle.

Meanwhile, let's deal with all those herbs. Combine the tarragon, dill, parsley and mint (or whichever combination you go with) on a board and chop finely. Place in a large jug and add the mustard, olive oil, vinegar, honey and some salt and pepper to taste, and whisk into a herby sludge (this also makes a great dressing for steamed green beans… just saying).

Transfer the warm potatoes to a container or serving bowl and pour the dressing and sliced apples over them. Gently toss to combine and finish with any extra herb leaves or edible flowers you have handy (the yellow flowers on page 131 came from our tarragon plant).

Travel advice
This potato salad is so easy to transport, mostly because it contains no mayonnaise or dairy. Just keep cool and sealed in its container. It's generally okay to leave it out at room temperature for an hour or so before serving.

• Pictured page 131

Pearled barley, pickled onion, walnut and roasted cauliflower salad

This is definitely a 'meal' salad in that there's so much going on, you could easily bring it as a stand-alone lunch. I'd just add some bread or crispbread and maybe some hard cheese to crumble over the top or serve alongside. Also, when making the pickled onions, please consider doubling the recipe as you might find they end up on nearly everything: great to pep up a big hearty curry, a toasted cheese sandwich, taco night, a simple rice bowl - anything.

Prep time 40 mins, plus pickling
Cook time 55 mins
Serves 6-8

1½ cups (300 g) pearled barley
2 Tbsp olive oil
1 cup (100 g) candied walnuts
  (see Note)

Pickled onions
3 red onions, thinly sliced
1½ Tbsp salt
2 Tbsp sugar
2 cups (500 ml) apple cider
  vinegar

Vegetables
1 small head broccoli, cut into
  small florets
½ head cauliflower, cut into
  small florets
¼ cup (60 ml) olive oil

Dressing
¼ cup (60 ml) extra virgin olive oil
½ tsp ground cumin
A pinch of cayenne pepper,
  or more if you'd like more heat
2 garlic cloves, finely chopped
Zest and juice of 1 lemon
2 Tbsp red wine vinegar
1 tsp sea salt
Lots of freshly ground black
  pepper

• *Pictured page 130*

For the pickled onions, pile the onion into one large jar or divide between two smaller ones. Combine the salt, sugar, vinegar and 1 cup (250 ml) water in a small saucepan over medium heat. Cook, stirring as you go, for a few minutes, or until the sugar and salt have dissolved.

Pour the hot mixture over your onions, pushing them down with the end of a wooden spoon so that everything is submerged. Seal and store in the fridge. These will be good to use after a few hours, but are best after a couple of days, and will last a few weeks in the fridge.

For the veggies, preheat the oven to 200°C (400°F) and combine the broccoli and cauliflower in a roasting tin. Drizzle with the olive oil, season with salt and pepper and roast for about 20 minutes, or until cooked through and beginning to caramelise.

To cook the barley, combine with the olive oil in a large saucepan over medium–high heat. Toast, stirring often, for 10 minutes, then pour in about 6 cups (1.5 litres) boiling water and cook over medium heat until tender, about 20 minutes (check after 15; the cooking time will depend on the freshness of your barley). Drain and set aside.

For the dressing, combine all the ingredients in a small bowl and whisk together. Check and adjust the seasoning to taste.

Tip the pearled barley (ideally it will still be hot or warm – this will help the grains soak up the dressing) into a large serving container or bowl. Top with the roasted veggies and add the dressing. Toss well so that everything is well mixed. Top with the candied walnuts, crushing them up into smaller pieces with your fingers as you go, then scatter with plenty of the pickled onions and you're ready to go! Yum.

Travel advice
Dress this salad early, as it just gets better with time. I think it's better at room temperature and not straight from the fridge. To keep the nuts crunchy and fresh, maybe scatter them on at the last minute.

Note
To make the candied walnuts, follow the recipe for the macadamia nuts on page 76 and add 1 tablespoon fennel seeds instead of the chilli. Or just use fresh or toasted walnuts.

Clockwise from left: Pearled barley, pickled onion, walnut and roasted cauliflower salad (page 129); Super herby potato salad (page 128); Coleslaw with green apples, bacon and buttermilk dressing (page 132)

Coleslaw with green apples, bacon and buttermilk dressing

This is a handy and quite light coleslaw. The lack of mayonnaise in the dressing won't be felt at all and, actually, the zing from the buttermilk, lemon and mustard is more than enough. Add in any extras you like here: shaved brussels sprouts and thinly sliced apple would be lovely, or any seasonal vegetable (or fruit) that can hold its crunch would also be welcome.

Prep time 15 mins
Cook time 15 mins
Serves 6–8

½ cup (50 g) flaked almonds
1 tsp olive oil
6 slices bacon, chopped into
    small pieces
½ white cabbage, finely
    shredded
2 tart green apples, cored
    and julienned

Dressing
¼ cup (60 ml) buttermilk
2 Tbsp dijon mustard
Juice of 1 lemon, or to taste
1 tsp honey

In a dry frying pan, toast the almonds over medium heat until golden brown then set aside. Add the oil to the pan, return to the heat, then fry the bacon until lovely and crispy.

Meanwhile, make the dressing by combining all the ingredients in a jar with some salt and pepper, give it a good shake and check the flavour. It might need a little more salt, pepper or lemon juice.

Combine the cabbage, apple, bacon and toasted almonds in a large bowl and add the dressing, tossing it through well.

Travel advice
Keep chilled and only mix in the dressing right before serving.

• *Pictured page 131*

Rocky road

A plate of rocky road will always be a winner. And, bonus: it's so easy to make!

1. Melt about 400 g (14 oz) of your favourite chocolate over a double-boiler or in the microwave.
2. Meanwhile, grease and line a 20 cm (8 inch) square cake tin with baking paper. Tip in 2 cups (180 g) torn up marshmallows, about 1 cup (40 g) broken pretzels or biscuits, and maybe some chopped Turkish delight, or any other sweets or nuts you fancy.
3. Pour the chocolate into the tin, pop in the fridge until set, then cut into pieces and share away!

White chocolate-dipped pretzels

More an idea than a recipe, and not even mine! My friend Amy often makes these for picnics and they are so, so moreish.

1. Just buy a packet of pretzels, melt some chocolate (white, milk or dark, whatever you prefer) and dip half a pretzel in the chocolate then place on a baking tray lined with baking paper.
2. Sprinkle with hundreds and thousands and pop in the fridge for the chocolate to harden up.
3. Store the pretzels in a jar or tin, share around and watch them disappear.

Travel advice
These travel well in an airtight container lined with baking paper. Keep the rocky road well chilled until you're ready to serve.

Things on bread, but make it fancy

I know – we're not reinventing the wheel here. Rather, reminding ourselves how wonderful 'good things on bread' are.

Tasty, crunchy, bright things piled on toasted slices of crusty bread and sliced then shared around is by far the easiest and often most economical way to entertain groups. So next time you're invited to bring nibbles, a starter or something to share around, why not buy a nice loaf, toast it till golden and top with one of the following options?

Oh, and if you live anywhere near a forest, or can get to one, there's a Japanese expression, shinrin-yoku, which translates as forest bathing. The idea, I think, is that you just explore the forest, letting your senses be your guide. May I suggest packing your bruschetta elements up and heading out for a spot of forest bathing followed by snacks as per the photos on page 136?

Nanae Harada and Robbie Robinson are experts in both forest bathing and foraging, and spend much of every autumn padding about the floor of the Mount Canobolas State Conservation Area collecting saffron milk cap mushrooms for local restaurants and markets. Sometimes they pack a little picnic and share the spoils of their forest bath with friends, which surely is the definition of a simple pleasure. Here are some tips and recipes from Nanae and me that you might like to try.

About the bread

For any bruschetta-style situation, you need to start with really good bread. Whether that's sliced sourdough, crunchy focaccia (my preference and what you see here – see pages 94–5 for my recipe), or baguettes sliced in half lengthways and lightly toasted, you need good bread slicked with good olive oil and cooked until crunchy.

Peach, cheddar and thyme bruschetta

Serves 3–4 Try this delicious combination on toasted bread, atop a focaccia (prior to cooking) or as a side dish for barbecued pork chops. Slice 3 ripe peaches and place in a bowl with 150 g (5½ oz) crumbled sharp cheddar and 2 teaspoons lemon thyme leaves. Drizzle in a couple of tablespoons of extra virgin olive oil and gently toss with your hands. Leave to come to room temperature for an hour or so before piling on your toasted bread.

Prosciutto, orange zest and burrata bruschetta

Serves 3–4 Burrata is a semi-soft cheese made from mozzarella and filled with cream. It's basically a cheese and sauce in one and, torn over crusty bread with prosciutto, is heaven. You can swap in mozzarella, bocconcini or even soft goat's cheese or feta – just ensure you bring the cheese out of the fridge about 20 minutes before assembly so the flavour can really shine. Tear 300 g (10½ oz) of the burrata, or whatever you're using, into small pieces and place in a bowl. Tear in 8 slices of prosciutto. Drizzle in a couple of tablespoons of fruity extra virgin olive oil, grate in the zest of an orange and sprinkle with chilli flakes. Leave this mixture for about half an hour or so before piling on your toasted bread.

Grated fig and chive bruschetta

Serves 3–4 Slice the stems from 3–4 figs. Place a box grater over a bowl and, using the biggest holes, grate your figs into a puddle of pink deliciousness. Stir in 1 tablespoon balsamic vinegar, 1 tablespoon or so of finely chopped chives and a pinch of salt and pepper. Spread on the toasted bread, top with some extra chopped chives and serve.

Travel advice
Pack your toasted bread and toppings in airtight containers. Chill the toppings but remove them 20 minutes before serving. Warm the bread on a fire or barbecue before topping.

Miso mushroom bruschetta

Nanae's miso butter is one of the most useful things you can have in the fridge, and this recipe makes quite a bit more than needed for that reason. A nicely wrapped log of it makes a gorgeous present for a friend, and it's divine smeared on a good steak just as it comes off the grill, tossed through steamed vegetables, spooned into a baked potato or just spread on good bread and topped with a pickle or two.

Prep time 10 mins
Cook time 15 mins
Serves 4

Miso butter
1 cup (250 g) unsalted butter,
   at room temperature
25 g (1 oz) miso (see Note)

Mushroom bruschetta
1 Tbsp olive oil
30 g (1 oz) Miso butter (see Note)
4 cups (400 g) wild mushrooms,
   such as saffron milk caps, or
   a mix of whichever ones look
   good at the shops
4 slices crusty bread
2 Tbsp chopped flat-leaf parsley
   leaves
Pickled radishes (see page 188)

For the miso butter, combine both ingredients in a bowl and mix until creamy. Form into a log shape, wrap tightly in plastic wrap and refrigerate until hard.

To make the bruschetta, heat the olive oil with half of the miso butter in a pan over medium–high heat.

Slice the mushrooms and add to the pan, tossing around gently to cook, for about 5–7 minutes or until wilted. Remove the mushrooms and set aside. Reduce the heat to medium. Add the remaining miso butter to the pan and now press the bread slices onto the hot surface, frying them for about 2 minutes each side or until golden.

Transfer to a plate, pile the mushrooms on top and sprinkle with parsley. Finish with a little pile of pickles.

Travel advice
Pack the miso butter, pickles, parsley and bread separately, then assemble on arrival – fry up your mushrooms once foraged (or pulled from your chiller bag) and assemble the bruschetta while they're still hot.

Note
I use Nanae's home-made miso, which we source from the Orange Farmers' Market. The better quality miso you use here, the better the end result will be – same goes for the butter, of course.

Biscuits for the tin

I aspire to always have a tin or jar of biscuits at the ready. And while this doesn't always eventuate, when it does I feel peak smugness! It's pretty great to have something to casually pull out when people 'pop in' (gah). Or to throw in the picnic basket for an outing.

These biscuits are just the kind of thing you might take to a picnic, take camping or present, dressed up in a cute jar with a ribbon around the top, as a thank-you gift.

I also think a plate of biscuits, the one kind or a mixture, with some fresh seasonal fruit, maybe some nice chocolate, makes a wonderful dessert. There's no plating up, no washing up and everyone can just pick and choose what they fancy.

And if you don't have time to make your biscuits, just go and buy some nice ones and package them up in a jar - whatever works, works!

Orange and rhubarb melting moments

You can never ever go wrong with a good melting moment. They really do seem to delight everyone, especially with such a pretty pink filling. I like to cook mine a little longer than most recipes suggest so they don't go soggy or too soft. Either way, if you haven't made these before, or for a while, please give them a go. They're such a lovely thing to bring to a picnic, or anywhere. Once the filling is firm and set, they are pretty shelf-stable for a couple of days at least.

Prep time 20 mins, plus chilling
Cook time 15 mins
Makes approx. 24

1 cup (250 g) unsalted butter,
   at room temperature
80 g (2¾ oz) icing
   (confectioners') sugar
Zest of 1 orange
1 tsp vanilla paste
⅓ cup (50 g) custard powder
1⅔ cups (250 g) plain
   (all-purpose) flour
A pinch of salt

Filling
100 g (3½ oz) butter, softened
2 cups (250 g) icing
   (confectioners') sugar
3 Tbsp rhubarb or plum jam
1 Tbsp orange juice, plus extra
   if needed

Place the butter and sugar in the bowl of a stand mixer fitted with the paddle attachment and cream for a few minutes until pale and fluffy. Or you can use a large bowl and an electric mixer. Add the zest and vanilla and beat again. Fold in the custard powder, flour and salt. Turn the dough out onto your benchtop and divide in two, then form each half into a sausage shape. Wrap in plastic wrap and refrigerate for at least 30 minutes.

Preheat the oven to 170°C (325°F) and line two baking trays with baking paper.

Slice each sausage of dough into discs around 1 cm (½ inch) thick, and roll these into small balls. Place these on the baking trays, leaving a few centimetres (about 1 inch) between each to allow for spreading. Gently press down with the tines of a fork to flatten a little.

Bake for 15 minutes, or until pale golden. Remove from the oven and leave to cool on a wire rack.

Meanwhile, clean the mixing bowl ready to make the filling. Combine the butter and sugar in the bowl of your stand mixer, or using a bowl and an electric mixer, and beat for a few minutes until pale and creamy. Add the jam and the 1 tablespoon of orange juice and mix again until you have a thick paste. Add more orange juice if needed, a little at a time, until you have the right consistency.

Sandwich two biscuits together with a little of the filling and place in the fridge for the buttercream filling to set, then store in an airtight container for up to 2 days.

Travel advice
If you're making these biscuits more than 3 days in advance, store them, unfilled, in an airtight container and then sandwich together on the day you plan to share them.

• *Pictured page 138*

Dark chocolate tahini biscuits

The tahini in this recipe is barely noticeable, but it balances the sweetness with its inherent savoury flavour, making these biscuits that much more delicious. You could swap it with peanut butter if you prefer, or if you don't have tahini. Either way, these biscuits are at their best when the dough has had a day or two in the fridge before baking. Or a couple of hours at least. This means you can have them rolled and ready to bake up to 5 days ahead and bake beautiful, hot biscuits on demand.

Prep time 20 mins, plus chilling
Cook time 15–20 mins
Makes approx. 24

100 g (3½ oz) unsalted butter, at room temperature
100 g (3½ oz) tahini
60 g (2 oz) caster (superfine) sugar
½ cup (110 g) brown sugar
2 eggs
1 tsp vanilla paste
A pinch of sea salt, plus extra to serve
1⅓ cups (200 g) plain (all-purpose) flour
1 tsp baking powder
200 g (7 oz) good-quality dark chocolate (minimum 70% cocoa), roughly chopped

Combine the butter, tahini and sugars in the bowl of a stand mixer fitted with the paddle attachment. Alternatively, just use a large bowl and an electric mixer. Cream together until pale and fluffy, then add the eggs, one at a time, beating well between each addition.

Fold in the vanilla, salt, flour and baking powder, then finally fold in the chocolate. Roll the dough into around 24 balls, each about the size of a walnut, and place on a tray or in a container. Cover and pop in the fridge for at least 2 hours, but up to 2 days.

When ready to bake, line two trays with baking paper and preheat the oven to 180°C (350°F). Bake the biscuits for 15–20 minutes or until risen and pale golden. Sprinkle with a little more sea salt and leave to cool. Store in an airtight container for up to a week.

Travel advice
Once completely cool, it is best to store these in an airtight container on their own away from other softer biscuits, as they will absorb their moisture and lose their crunch.

• Pictured page 143

Jammy macaroons

While I find the almond meal-based macaron quite fussy and fiddly to make, its coconutty cousin, the macaroon, is so easy, and just as delicious. If not more so. I've made these in a sort of jam-drop shape, but you could leave out the jam and drizzle with dark chocolate instead.

Prep time 20 mins
Cook time 50 mins
Makes approx. 12

1½ cups (135 g) desiccated coconut
2 egg whites
½ cup (110 g) caster (superfine) sugar
1 tsp vanilla paste
2 Tbsp almond meal
⅓ cup (110 g) rhubarb jam, or similar

Preheat the oven to 180°C (350°F). Toast the coconut on a baking tray in the oven for 15 minutes, or until pale golden. Leave to cool completely.

Reduce the oven temperature to 150°C (300°F). Line two trays with baking paper.

Place the egg whites in the bowl of a stand mixer fitted with the whisk attachment and whisk to firm peaks. Or you can use a large bowl and an electric mixer. Add the sugar, a little at a time, until completely incorporated into a glossy meringue.

Gently, by hand but using the whisk attachment, incorporate the vanilla, toasted (and cooled) coconut and the almond meal.

You can either spoon the mixture onto your trays (about 1 tablespoon at a time), or transfer to a piping bag and pipe neat mounds. Either way, leave a little space between each to allow for spreading. Then, dip your finger into a glass of water and make a little indent in the top of each biscuit. Fill this with the jam (no more than ½ teaspoon or it will run and spread).

Place in the oven to bake for about 35 minutes, or until pale golden. Let them cool on their trays then store in an airtight container for up to a week.

Fruity nutty oat biscuits

We can definitely put these in the 'biscuits for breakfast' category. I can also attest to the fact that they taste good with a slice of sharp, crumbly cheddar and a thin slice of pear.

Prep time 20 mins, plus chilling
Cook time 15–30 mins
Makes approx. 24

220 g (7¾ oz) unsalted butter, at room temperature
⅔ cup (150 g) brown sugar
130 g (4¾ oz) caster (superfine) sugar
2 eggs
1 tsp vanilla paste
1 tsp bicarbonate of soda (baking soda)
1 tsp ground allspice
A pinch of salt
1⅓ cups (200 g) plain (all-purpose) flour
150 g (5½ oz) dried mixed fruit (I use a mixture of dried apricots and figs, fairly finely chopped)
1 cup (100 g) rolled oats
150 g (5½ oz) hazelnuts, roasted and roughly chopped

Preheat the oven to 180°C (350°F) and line two baking trays with baking paper.

Place the butter and sugars in the bowl of a stand mixer fitted with the paddle attachment, or use a large bowl and an electric mixer, and beat until pale and creamy. Add the eggs, one at a time, beating well between each addition.

Fold in the vanilla, bicarbonate of soda, allspice, salt and flour, then the fruit, oats and hazelnuts.

Roll tablespoons of the mixture into balls and place on the trays, leaving space for spreading. If you're working in batches, return the biscuit mixture to the fridge between each round.

Bake for 15–20 minutes or until golden brown. Leave to cool on a wire rack then store in an airtight container for up to a week. If the bases of your biscuits are still a bit soft after they've cooled, just pop them back in the oven for another 5–10 minutes.

From left: Jammy macaroons; Dark chocolate tahini biscuits (page 141); Fruity nutty oat biscuits

Celebration cakes

Sometimes you need to bring out the big guns. To go the extra mile and make something quite special – a cake that says I think you're worth half a day. Worth all that washing up. Worth layers and buttercream and a bit of faff.

We all need a few celebration cake recipes to fall back on, and these are the ones I always love most. They are all properly delicious and, when you break them down, not at all hard to make (though I think they look impressive).

And the best bit? You only need one (maybe two) of these in your repertoire – cakes that become family favourites and traditions. Cakes that are made on repeat, year after year, that become part of your family's fabric. Cakes like these.

Chocolate orange layer cake with chocolate buttercream

If you are a fan of Jaffa Cakes, then you will love this deep, dark, orange-and-chocolate cake as much as I do. And when sandwiched with this sensational buttercream, it really is a total winner. A grown-up, very rich birthday or celebration cake. A note on the buttercream: I owe this method to the clever team at Bourke Street Bakery who shared it in their book of the same name. It works like a dream and the way it comes together - almost like magic - always delights me. It's the small things.

Prep time 40 mins, plus chilling
Cook time 1 hour 15 mins
Serves 8–10

2 whole oranges
200 g (7 oz) dark chocolate (minimum 70% cocoa), roughly chopped
220 g (7¾ oz) plain (all-purpose) flour
40 g (1½ oz) cocoa powder
200 g (7 oz) caster (superfine) sugar
100 g (3½ oz) brown sugar
A pinch of salt
2 tsp baking powder
½ cup (125 ml) vegetable oil
3 eggs, lightly beaten
1 tsp vanilla paste
250 g (9 oz) sour cream
½ cup (125 ml) espresso coffee, cooled

Buttercream
200 ml (7 fl oz) single (pure) cream
1 Tbsp cocoa powder
Zest of 1 orange
100 g (3½ oz) caster (superfine) sugar
200 g (7 oz) dark chocolate (minimum 70% cocoa), roughly chopped
300 g (10½ oz) unsalted butter, cubed

Start with the buttercream. Heat the cream, cocoa powder, orange zest and sugar in a saucepan over medium heat and bring to the boil, whisking as you go. Boil for 1 minute, then remove from the heat and stir in the chocolate and butter. Return to a low heat and whisk until the butter has melted completely. Pour the mixture into a mixing bowl and place in the fridge to chill for at least 2 hours.

Place the oranges in a saucepan of cold water. Bring to the boil and cook for about 30 minutes or until completely soft. Remove from the water, roughly chop and transfer to a blender or food processor to blitz to a purée. Set aside to cool for at least 20 minutes before making the rest of the batter.

Melt the chocolate in a heatproof bowl set over a saucepan of simmering water, or using a microwave, and set aside to cool while getting the rest of the batter together.

Preheat the oven to 180°C (350°F) and grease and line two 20 cm (8 inch) cake tins.

Place the flour, cocoa powder, sugars, salt and baking powder in a bowl and whisk to combine. In a separate large bowl, whisk together the oil, eggs, vanilla, sour cream and coffee until well combined.

Pour the wet ingredients into the dry ingredients, add the orange purée and melted chocolate, and stir until smooth.

Divide the cake batter between the two tins and bake for 30 minutes or until a skewer inserted in the middle of the cakes comes out clean. Leave to cool for 10 minutes before turning out onto a wire rack to cool completely. Once cool, halve the cakes to create four cake layers.

This is the fun bit. Pour the buttercream mixture into the bowl of a stand mixer fitted with the whisk attachment and whip for 2 minutes until pale, light and fluffy. Or use a large bowl and an electric mixer for this. Spread one-quarter of the buttercream over one cake half and sandwich with the other cake half. Repeat, spreading the last of the buttercream across the top and side of the cake, if you like.

Travel advice
If kept cool, this cake will hold together nicely. I would store it in the fridge before heading out to make sure the buttercream has 'set'.

Jam roll, raspberry and dark chocolate cake

This cake is very special to sisters Angela, Laura and Heidi. It comes out at engagement parties, birthday parties - all the parties - and is beloved by everyone. I love how families develop these conventions - unwritten rules for gathering that they just adhere to without question. So, if your parties are in need of a show stopper of a cake, Ehren, Angela's husband, has generously offered up his to share.

Prep time 20 mins, plus chilling
Cook time 5 mins
Serves 8-10

4 × 250 g (9 oz) packs mini jam rolls (Ehren uses vanilla and jam, but you could use chocolate if you prefer)
2 cups (300 g) frozen raspberries
1½ cups (375 ml) espresso coffee, cooled
1 cup (250 ml) sherry (or your favourite tipple; brandy would also be good here)
2 cups (500 ml) single (pure) cream
250 g (9 oz) dark chocolate (minimum 70% cocoa), roughly chopped

Take a 24 cm (9½ inch) springform cake tin and line the base with the mini jam rolls, all standing up to attention. Squash them in tightly and fill the gaps with the raspberries. Pour the coffee and sherry over the rolls, soaking them evenly.

Make a ganache by heating 1 cup (250 ml) of the cream in a small saucepan until just simmering. Remove from the heat and add most of the chocolate (save a few squares to grate over at the end). Stir until it melts into a glossy, thick sauce.

Pour the warm ganache over the rolls so that it evenly coats the 'cake'. This will act as the glue that keeps everything together. Plus, it's delicious. Place the cake in the fridge to set for at least 3 hours, or overnight. Just before serving, whip the remaining cream and spread over the cake in an even-ish layer. Grate the remaining chocolate over the cake and serve.

Travel advice
Once the cake has set in the fridge, it should be pretty easy to transport (chilled). If taking this any distance, whip the cream and grate the chocolate before setting off and transport these in separate containers (also chilled), then assemble on arrival.

Spiced hot chocolate

I've had Laura's spiced hot chocolate a few times at her cafe Nest, in Tumbarumba, and it's the best thing for a cold evening. I love to take it in a thermos to autumn picnics, plus biscuits for dipping.

1. Combine about 800 ml (28 fl oz) full-cream milk, 1 vanilla pod (seeds scraped), 1 cinnamon stick, 2 bruised cardamom pods and 1 halved and seeded hot red chilli, to taste, in a heavy-based saucepan and bring just to simmering point.
2. Grate in 200 g (7 oz) dark chocolate (minimum 70% cocoa) and stir. Turn off the heat and let it sit for 15 minutes, then fish out the spices and serve hot with a dusting of cinnamon.

Travel advice
Keep warm in a thermos or reheat over a hotplate.

Hazelnut meringue stack

This is proper dinner party birthday cake territory. It's a definite crowd pleaser, and even though there are a few steps in making it, they're not tricky and can all be done in advance. It's the cake my son has asked for as his birthday cake the last couple of years. Try to make this in stages over a couple of days so it's not a big production on the day. And speaking of stages, if you don't have time for all of them, the mousse on its own is a wondrous thing and perfect to take along to a birthday party with cold cream.

Prep time 40 mins, plus chilling
Cook time 1 hour 5 mins
Serves 8–10

Chocolate mousse
400 g (14 oz) good-quality dark chocolate (minimum 70% cocoa), roughly chopped
6 eggs, separated
1 cup (250 ml) single (pure) cream

Meringue
200 g (7 oz) hazelnuts, skin on
8 egg whites
360 g (12¾ oz) caster (superfine) sugar
1 tsp white vinegar

To assemble
1 cup (250 ml) single (pure) cream
200 g (7 oz) raspberries
50 g (1¾ oz) good-quality dark chocolate (minimum 70% cocoa), grated

Start by making the mousse. Melt the chocolate in the microwave or over a double-boiler and set aside to cool for a few minutes.

Place the egg yolks into the bowl of a stand mixer fitted with the whisk attachment, or use a large bowl and an electric mixer, and whip until pale and fluffy. Transfer to a mixing bowl.

Pour the cream into your stand mixer bowl (I don't bother cleaning it as everything gets mixed together anyway), then whisk to soft peaks. Gently fold into the whipped yolks.

Clean and dry the stand mixer bowl thoroughly (this time the bowl has to be spotless as any residue will stop the whites from whipping properly). Add the egg whites and whisk to stiff peaks.

Gently fold the melted chocolate into the whipped yolk and cream mixture and, finally, fold in the whipped egg whites. You want to just bring everything together while losing minimal air. Refrigerate for a few hours to set.

To make the meringue, preheat the oven to 150°C (300°F). Spread the nuts on a baking tray and toast for 10 minutes. As soon as they come out of the oven, tip onto a large tea towel, gather the edges together and rub to remove the skins.

Transfer your now-skinned nuts to a food processor or mortar and pestle and pulse or bash to a fine crumb.

Now take four trays and line them with baking paper. If you don't have four trays or don't have room for four trays in your oven (me), then either make in batches (the mixture should hold up okay between baking) or just do two layers. Trace out a 20 cm (8 inch) circle on the underside of each piece of baking paper.

Place the egg whites in the cleaned and dried bowl of your stand mixer and whisk to stiff peaks. Add the sugar, 1 tablespoon at a time, until all combined, then whisk for 2 minutes. Now, by hand, gently stir the vinegar and hazelnuts into the meringue mixture.

Spoon about one-quarter of the mixture onto one of the lined trays, smoothing it out into the 20 cm (8 inch) circle, then repeat with the remaining mixture and trays.

If your oven can fit the four trays at once, bake them all together for 45 minutes. Otherwise, bake them two at a time. Transfer the meringue discs to a wire rack to cool.

When you're ready to assemble the stack, whip the cream to soft peaks. Place one of the meringue discs on a cake stand or plate and spread it with half the cream. Place another disc on top and spread it with half the chocolate mousse. Repeat, finishing with the raspberries and grated chocolate.

Refrigerate the stack for at least half an hour before serving to make it easier to cut.

Variations
• Swap the hazelnuts with almonds, walnuts or pecans.
• Fold ½ cup (50 g) grated dark chocolate into the meringue mixture with the nuts.
• Use white or milk chocolate instead of dark if you prefer.
• Instead of finishing with raspberries, use any seasonal fruit. Sliced mangoes would be lovely in summer, or beautiful ripe peaches.

Travel advice
If this needs to 'keep' for more than a couple of hours, travel first and assemble later. Keep the meringue layers wrapped tightly in plastic wrap, and the mousse and cream chilled.

Plum and ricotta crostata

I spent a few years living in Italy in my twenties and during this time I fell for crostata in all its forms. I loved how whenever there was a dinner party or gathering, my friends would stop on the way at a pasticceria to buy a beautifully wrapped crostata to give to the host. It's just the thing to take to a celebration of any kind. Delicious on the day and also excellent as breakfast the day after, or perhaps your host might like to take some to work for morning tea and share around? Either way, crostata keeps nicely for a few days and makes a lovely gift.

Prep time 25 mins, plus resting
Cook time 40 mins
Serves 8–10

1 cup (320 g) plum jam or other jam of your choice (apricot and blackberry are my favourites; quince is amazing, too)
¼ cup (55 g) caster (superfine) sugar

Pastry
1⅔ cups (250 g) plain (all-purpose) flour
100 g (3½ oz) icing (confectioners') sugar
1 tsp grated lemon zest
1 tsp baking powder
A pinch of salt
½ cup (125 g) cold butter, cubed
1 egg
1 egg yolk

Ricotta filling
1 cup (230 g) fresh ricotta
¼ cup (30 g) icing (confectioners') sugar
1 vanilla pod, seeds scraped
3 eggs

To make the pastry, combine the flour, sugar, lemon zest, baking powder and salt in a bowl. Tip onto a work surface and add the butter, rubbing it into the flour with your fingertips until the mixture resembles coarse sand (with a few small pebbles). Add the egg and yolk and, using a light hand, bring the mixture together until you have a smooth dough (it's okay if there are some streaks of butter). Form into a disc, wrap in plastic wrap and rest in the fridge for 30 minutes.

For the filling, whisk together all the ingredients until well combined. Place the jam in a small saucepan and gently heat, then set aside. Preheat the oven to 180°C (350°F).

To roll out the crostata, first cut away about one-third of the pastry and roll out the remaining two-thirds until you have a large disc about 4 mm (³⁄₁₆ inch) thick. Gently transfer the pastry into a 22 cm (8½ inch) fluted, loose-bottomed tart tin (or a springform cake tin will be fine, too, in which case you will want to trim the edges of your pastry first so they are relatively even).

Trim any excess pastry, leaving a 1 cm (½ inch) border and fold this down into the edge of the tin to 'reinforce' the crostata's side. Spoon the ricotta mixture onto the base of the pastry and top with dollops of jam. Roll out the remaining pastry and cut into about ten strips. Arrange five of these across the top of the tart and then spin it around and crisscross the remaining five strips in a lattice pattern on the other side, weaving the strips over and under each other.

Trim any excess pastry, sprinkle with the caster sugar and bake for 35 minutes or until the pastry is golden brown.

Serve warm or chilled (if you're serving it chilled, you'll find it slices much more cleanly).

Travel advice
Once cooled, this crostata is a pretty good traveller. Just pop it in a tray or container so it can't roll around the back of the car and it should be fine.

Dinner for the camping trip

Okay. So, you're going camping. It's a whole thing. Everyone's super organised with spreadsheets of who's bringing what and you've been assigned two dinners. Here are four options.

The pearled barley bake, chickpeas and gratin will all offer a nice, meat-free change after all those sausages in bread rolls. And/or will sit happily alongside them.

And the lamb shanks are genuinely one of the best things I've ever eaten al fresco. Al anywhere. Thank you to Amanda Thomas for this recipe. It's a genuine crowd pleaser, especially when served with buttered damper rolls and those fried potatoes.

Whatever you bring, though, remember that all food tastes better outside, by a fire, under the stars, so don't stress. Keep it simple, and happy camping!

Baked pearled barley with all the early autumn veggies

This recipe does a few things well: firstly, it uses a heap of the beautiful vegetables in season around early autumn (think zucchini/courgette, tomato, corn and eggplant/aubergine). Next, it feeds a load of people in one tasty package. And, finally, it's not at all hard to throw together and doesn't mind being left out at room temperature for a while (within reason). One more - it's almost tastier as leftovers reheated with buttered toast.

Prep time 20 mins
Cook time 1 hour 40 mins
Serves 6–8 as a side

1 cup (200 g) pearled barley
¼ cup (60 ml) olive oil
1 brown onion, diced
3 garlic cloves, finely chopped
2 zucchini (courgettes), cut into
    2 cm (¾ inch) cubes
2 ears of corn, kernels cut off
3 medium tomatoes, diced
1 eggplant (aubergine), cut into
    2 cm (¾ inch) cubes
2 cups (500 ml) tomato passata
    (puréed tomatoes)
1 handful basil leaves
1 cup (60 g) chunky
    breadcrumbs
1 cup (100 g) freshly grated
    parmesan
1 cup (130 g) mozzarella, torn
    into rough pieces

Rinse the pearled barley until the water runs clear then place in a saucepan and fill with cold water. Bring to the boil and cook for about 25 minutes, or until al dente, then drain.

Heat half the olive oil in a deep-sided ovenproof frying pan and cook the onion for about 15 minutes, or until completely soft and beginning to caramelise. Add the garlic and cook for a few more minutes. Remove the onion and garlic from the pan and set aside.

Return the pan to the heat, add a splash more oil, increase the heat to high and fry the zucchini and corn kernels until softened and starting to colour, about 10 minutes. Transfer these to the dish with the onion. Add a splash more oil and fry the tomatoes and eggplant for about 10 minutes.

Preheat the oven to 200°C (400°F).

Return all of the vegetables to the frying pan and add the passata with ½ cup (125 ml) water and the basil leaves, then stir to combine. Season well with salt and black pepper. Add the barley to the pan and stir to combine.

Sprinkle with the breadcrumbs and cheese, and bake for 30 minutes or until the top is golden and crunchy.

Travel advice
Cover tightly with foil to keep warm, and rest easy knowing that this will sit happily at room temperature for a reasonable amount of time, getting more and more delicious while it waits for you. You can also make it a couple of days in advance and keep it chilled, then reheat it on arrival or serve at room temperature.

Spicy confit chickpeas

This is another winner if your remit is to bring something substantial, meat-free, good to eat over a few days and jam-packed with flavour. Also, it's basically a stir-then-dump in the oven or barbecue situation and what comes out 2 hours later is the most moreish, spicy, almost jammy chickpea confit. Great as a side dish with grilled meats, or you could spread onto bruschetta, serve in little bowls with a poached egg slipped on top or thin out with stock and have as a soup. It's also quite rich and packs a lot of flavour so a little goes a long way.

Prep time 10 mins
Cook time 2 hours
Serves 6–8 as a side

3 cups (600 g) chickpeas, cooked (see Note)
8 large garlic cloves, peeled
800 g (1 lb 12 oz) tin whole cherry tomatoes
250 g (9 oz) fresh cherry tomatoes
1 Tbsp sambal oelek
1 Tbsp smoked paprika
75 ml (2½ fl oz) olive oil
150 g (5½ oz) feta cheese, crumbled
2 Tbsp roughly chopped parsley leaves
Juice of 1 lemon, or to taste

Preheat the oven to 140°C (275°F). Combine the chickpeas, garlic, tinned and fresh tomatoes, sambal oelek, paprika and olive oil in a large ovenproof saucepan or dish.

Mix together well, cover with a lid and place in the oven for 2 hours, stirring a few times along the way.

Once everything has cooked down into an aromatic, almost jammy confit, remove the dish from the oven and transfer the chickpea mixture to a serving bowl or container. This is divine either hot, straight out of the oven, or at room temperature.

Right before serving, stir through the feta and sprinkle with the parsley. Squeeze some lemon juice over, to taste.

Travel advice

This will keep beautifully at room temperature for a few hours but if you're travelling a distance or making it up a day or two in advance, chill until just before lunch or dinner. If you'd like to have this hot and don't mind the weight, transport in the oven dish or even your slow-cooker wrapped in a towel.

Note

You can use dried chickpeas that have been soaked overnight before being cooked, or simply use tinned cooked chickpeas, drained and rinsed well.

Cannellini bean, fennel and garlic gratin

I'm extra happy with this recipe. It's been a hit on cold nights with a green salad, on paddock picnics as a bed for barbecued sausages, as a stand-alone meal, and in a basket to deliver to friends in need of something nourishing, easy and filling to eat. It's handy, helpful and, most importantly, really tasty. For camping, just pack all the elements separately and cook on site. Ideally there'll be an oven, a camp oven or a barbecue with a lid but, at a pinch, a hotplate will do the job.

Prep time 15 mins
Cook time 3 hours
Serves 6–8

3 cups (585 g) dried cannellini
  beans, soaked overnight
⅓ cup (80 ml) olive oil
1 Tbsp sea salt
2 brown onions, peeled and
  quartered
1 large fennel bulb, trimmed and
  cut into eighths (reserve fronds
  for later)
4 garlic cloves, unpeeled
2 cups (500 ml) chicken stock or
  water
2 Tbsp thyme leaves
1 cup (100 g) grated cheddar
Focaccia (see pages 94–5),
  or crusty bread
Rocket (arugula), to serve

Drain, then rinse the beans and place in a large saucepan. Fill with enough water to cover the beans by 3 cm (1¼ inches). Add a couple of tablespoons of the olive oil and the salt. Cover and bring to the boil, then reduce the heat as low as possible and cook for 1–2 hours, or until the beans are tender but not falling apart. Drain and set aside.

Preheat the oven to 200°C (400°F).

Place the onion and fennel in a large ovenproof frying pan. Bash the garlic cloves with the side of your knife and throw them in the pan too. Pour in the rest of the olive oil and season well. Toss together then roast for about 40 minutes, or until the onions, fennel and garlic are completely soft and beginning to caramelise.

Smoosh the garlic cloves out of their skins and stir the garlic flesh into the fennel mixture. Add the beans, stock or water and thyme leaves. Gently stir and return to the oven for another 40 minutes, or until you are happy with how it's all looking (it should be golden, bubbly and the beans at the top will be starting to crisp up).

Scatter with the cheese and return to the oven for a final 10 minutes.

You could keep cooking this for a while longer so the liquid reduces right down, or serve it a bit more 'brothy'. I like the latter, and then dish it up with crunchy golden focaccia or crusty bread and a bowl of rocket. Scatter the reserved fennel fronds on top as garnish.

Travel advice
If you aren't going too far, keep at room temperature. This recipe is a pretty easygoing traveller; just keep it covered and wrapped tightly in a towel or tea towels and serve it at room temperature. You can also make it a couple of days in advance and keep it chilled, then reheat it on arrival or serve at room temperature.

Slow-cooked lamb shanks

This recipe tells the story of family gatherings out west by the Macquarie River, of glowing coals and big pots of steaming lamb stuffed into soft floury rolls, eaten fireside with a crowd. We were lucky enough to join the Thomas family of Warren, western New South Wales, on one of their recent cookouts and what came out of their camp oven was one of the best meals I've ever had. Thank you, Amanda, for sharing your recipe and camp-oven tips.

Prep time 45 mins
Cook time Light the fire 2–3 hours prior to cooking, then cooking time varies from 2–4 hours depending on how attentive your fire captain is. If cooking this in a regular oven at home, it will take about 2 hours at 140°C (275°F).
Serves 15 adults + a fair few kids

1½ cups (225 g) plain (all-purpose) flour, to coat
2 tsp salt
2 tsp freshly ground black pepper
12 lamb shanks
½ cup (125 ml) olive oil
2 brown onions, diced
6 garlic cloves, finely chopped
2 carrots, diced
2 celery stalks, diced
2 rosemary sprigs, leaves roughly chopped
1 cup (250 ml) red wine
800 g (1 lb 12 oz) tin crushed tomatoes
2 Tbsp tomato paste (concentrated purée)
4 cups (1 litre) chicken stock
1 Tbsp gravy powder
Cornflour (cornstarch), to thicken
Bread rolls and good butter, to serve

Before leaving home

If you're making these for a camping trip or evening picnic with a campfire, get most of the prep out of the way before leaving home, starting with browning the shanks.

Season the flour with the salt and pepper and place in one large or two small bags. Place the shanks in your bag/s and dance around vigorously to evenly coat the shanks.

Heat a little of the oil in a large frying pan over high heat and brown the shanks in batches, allowing them about 4 minutes per side to make sure they're properly browned. Place the browned shanks in a large container and refrigerate.

Reduce the heat under the pan, add a little more olive oil and cook the onion, stirring often, for about 20 minutes or until soft and caramelised. Add the garlic and cook for a few more minutes. Now add the carrot, celery and rosemary leaves, and cook until the vegetables have softened, about another 20 minutes.

Place the cooked vegetables in a separate container and pop in the fridge with the lamb. Keep everything chilled until you're fireside and ready to cook.

Campsite activity

Have a designated 'fire captain' in the group and ask him or her to get the fire going at least 2 or 3 hours before you need to start cooking in order to have the finest-quality coals to come on this culinary journey with you.

Dig a hole about twice as wide and a little deeper than your camp oven (see page 166).

For the number of shanks in this recipe, Amanda suggests two camp ovens to make sure they each have the space they need to reach their full potential. If halving the recipe, one large camp oven should work.

Make sure the location of the hole is in a good spot: more than a few steps away from the main fire and not near any potholes or sticks that will try to jump up and grab you later when it's dark, and you're walking with a shovel of hot coals (trust me, it's a thing). >

What Can I Bring?

Slow-cooked lamb shanks, continued...

Getting started

If you haven't already done all the browning and cooking of the vegetables at home, get the fire captain to crank up the heat and lay the camp ovens on top of the coals. Let them warm, and then pour in a good few glugs of oil and brown the shanks and veggies as explained on page 164.

If you've already done that step, heat a little oil in the camp ovens and add the vegetables to warm.

Now divvy up the shanks and put them into the ovens. Add the wine and cook for a few minutes, stirring, so it reduces down. Now might be a good time to pour yourself a glass, too!

The remaining wet ingredients are added, bit by bit, on an 'as needed' basis. Start off with half the tomatoes, the tomato paste and half the stock. You want to cover everything but not drown it, so save a bit to add later based on how it's looking. We want a less-is-more approach here. Add plenty of salt and pepper, cover and relax for at least an hour or two.

Check the shanks every half an hour, giving everything a gentle stir with a big slotted spoon and adding some more tomatoes and stock depending on the liquid levels. Put the lid back on and chill out for another little while.

Prod the fire captain to replenish the coals every hour or two, telling them all the time that the fate of the feast depends on their attentiveness. There is no science with this, and you can't really overcook them, it's just a game of managing the liquid levels.

Towards the end, add the gravy powder and give it a good stir. You might need some more stock or water here if it's looking too thick. If you think you've overdone it with the liquid and it's all looking a bit runny, pull out the cornflour and make a paste using 1 tablespoon cornflour and some cold water in a cup, then stir the paste in and cook for another 20 minutes or so.

Serve with bread rolls spread with butter.

Travel advice

If you're browning and cooking the vegetables in advance, make sure the shanks especially are kept chilled right up until cooking. If making from scratch at the campsite, keep the meat chilled until cooking.

What is a camp oven?

A camp oven is a large cast-iron pot with a lid, which can be used to do everything from bake bread to slow-cook dinners as we are doing here. The most common way of cooking with them is to dig a hole, slightly larger than the oven, and fill it with hot coals, then place the camp oven in the hole, cover the lid with a few more coals and leave it to cook. If you don't have one handy, a Dutch oven will work well but perhaps not over the coals! You might need to place it on a shelf over the fire or cook at home and transport the food in an insulated thermal container.

Fried mixed potatoes

These potatoes are insanely good, especially cooked over coals and eaten fireside. Though isn't everything? Thank you again, Amanda.

Prep time 10 mins
Cook time Depends on the temperature of your camp oven. If making this on a barbecue or stovetop at home, allow about 35 minutes
Feeds 6–8 as a side dish

¼ cup (60 ml) vegetable oil
500 g (1 lb 2 oz) potatoes, peeled and cut into 3–4 cm (1¼–1½ inch) pieces
500 g (1 lb 2 oz) sweet potatoes, peeled and cut into 3–4 cm (1¼–1½ inch) pieces
4 Tbsp chopped rosemary leaves
1 Tbsp sea salt, or to taste

Heat the vegetable oil in the bottom of a camp oven over fairly hot coals, or in a frying pan over medium–high heat. Add the potato and sweet potato, ideally in one layer (if you are cooking for a crowd and can't fit them all in, use a second camp oven or pile them in more than one layer and lose a little crunch at the end but none of the deliciousness!).

Cover and cook for about 20 minutes, or until tender. Remove the lid, flip the potatoes to brown the other side, add the rosemary and salt and cook for another 10–15 minutes, uncovered.

Serve hot, with the lamb and perhaps the coleslaw from page 132.

Travel advice
Peel and cube the vegetables before setting off then store in an airtight container and keep chilled (don't worry if they brown up a bit), then pack the oil, herbs and salt separately and fry in a cast-iron pan (or similar) over a barbecue plate.

A family banquet

Big flavours, loads of texture, colour and love – this is cooking in the Saliba family. Especially in the kitchens of sisters Rachel, Michelle and Reanne.

All three live along the same road out of Gulgong in central western New South Wales, and between them they have ten children, three farms and an intertwined life where family catch-ups are a constant. Good food, usually home-grown and cooked as their Lebanese grandmother would have, underpins it all.

Rachel, the youngest, grows organic garlic on her property. Just down the road Michelle is farming and raising her own family, and a little further along is Reanne, the oldest sister, also a wonderful cook plus a talented ceramicist, creating platters and special pieces for her family to share their precious dishes on.

'This menu brings up so many memories of our Taitare (grandmother),' our host today, Rachel Saliba, tells me. 'Every time we'd get together as a family, she'd spend days preparing incredible feasts. Now my sisters and I split the cooking between the three of us. All of these recipes are a celebration of our grandmother and our Lebanese heritage.'

Menu

Feast.

Toum (Garlic dip)

This powerfully flavoured dip is incredible as a condiment with barbecued or roasted meats. It's also excellent tossed with steamed veggies, spread thinly on warm toast and topped with roasted asparagus, or wherever you fancy some garlicky goodness. Rachel explained that toum took pride of place at family dinners at her grandparents' when she was growing up. Now she's the lucky one who gets to provide the toum for family meals. Thank you, Rach, for sharing it with us.

Prep time 15 mins
Cook time NIL
Makes approx. 1½ cups (450 g)

400 ml (14 fl oz) sunflower oil, high oleic if possible
Juice of 1 lemon (about 40 ml/2 Tbsp)
70 g (2½ oz) good-quality fresh garlic, cloves peeled
1 tsp salt

Place the sunflower oil and lemon juice in the bowl of your food processor and hold the pulse button down for 30 seconds. Pour this emulsion into a jug; there's no need to clean the bowl.

Pulse the garlic and salt in the food processor until you have a fairly fine paste. You might need to stop and scrape down the side every now and then. Add a tiny bit of the lemon and oil emulsion to help with this if necessary.

Start the processor at medium speed and slowly add the emulsion so it drips evenly into the garlic and begins to bind. Continue until you have used all the emulsion. You should end up with a thick white sauce consistency; it will thicken further in the fridge.

Transfer to a sterile jar and keep in the fridge for up to 1 month. The flavour will develop and intensify over time.

Travel advice
Store in a jar and keep in an insulated ice box or cooler.

• *Pictured page 168*

Labne with crunchy vegetables

Labne is the very best of kitchen friends - all it asks for is two ingredients and some time. And in return, you get the most intensely tangy, sour, thick dip/spread/sauce. Here, Rachel has kept her recipe pretty simple because there's a lot of other goodness going on in our menu, but you could add some toasted spices, fold through freshly chopped herbs, or even roll the labne into balls (roll these in spices and then store them in a jar of olive oil in the fridge).

Prep time 10 mins, plus draining
Cook time NIL
Makes approx. 1½ cups (600 g)

1 kg (2 lb 4 oz) Greek-style yoghurt
2 tsp salt
Olive oil (optional), for drizzling
Smoked paprika (optional), to serve
Raw veggies, such as radishes, celery, carrot or
   cucumber, trimmed, peeled and sliced for dipping
Toasted pita bread, to serve

Combine the yoghurt and salt in a bowl and stir well.

Line a sieve with a muslin cloth or clean disposable cloth and suspend over a bowl. Pour the yoghurt and salt mixture into the lined sieve, gently tie the cloth corners together and leave in the fridge overnight for the yoghurt to drain and thicken.

Congratulations, you have now made labne! Remove from the muslin and transfer to a serving bowl or platter. Smooth out and drizzle with olive oil and/or smoked paprika. Serve with a mix of raw vegetables and perhaps some toasted pita bread.

Travel advice
Transport from the fridge in an airtight container or wide-mouthed jar and keep in an insulated ice box or cooler.

• *Pictured page 168*

Lamb koftas

This is Reanne's recipe, something she often cooks for her four children and extended family. Try the kofta straight off the barbecue, squeezed into warm pita bread with hummus and a side of Fattoush (page 175) and maybe a little Toum (see opposite) on top just to gild the lily. Picnic food just got a major flavour injection.

Prep time 10 mins, plus chilling
Cook time 10–15 mins
Makes approx. 15 skewers

1 kg (2 lb 4 oz) minced (ground) lamb
1 brown onion, finely diced
2 cups (40 g) parsley leaves, finely chopped
2 Tbsp Lebanese spice mix (see Note)
2½ tsp salt
1 tsp ground black pepper

Combine all the ingredients in a large bowl and mix together well.

Shape the kofta mix into about 15 sausage-shaped pieces, about 10 × 3 cm (4 × 1¼ inches). Pierce lengthways with metal or wooden skewers (soaked in water for a few hours beforehand), then pile on a tray, cover tightly and keep chilled for up to 1 day.

Cook the skewers on a barbecue grill or in a frying pan over high heat for about 5 minutes on each side or until cooked through. Keep warm while you cook them all, then serve in a big pile with lots of hummus and Lebanese bread.

Travel advice
You can cook these in advance and keep them chilled then serve cold or have them made up and transport to your gathering chilled, ready to barbecue and share hot on the spot. If it's the latter, be sure to transport in an insulated ice box or cooler with plenty of ice bricks to keep the uncooked meat at a safe temperature (under 5°C/41°F). I'd play it safe and freeze them then transport straight from the freezer so they can thaw safely in the cooler.

Note
To make a Lebanese spice mix, combine the following ingredients and keep in a jar or airtight container: 1 tablespoon ground allspice, 1 tablespoon ground coriander, 1 tablespoon ground cinnamon, 1½ teaspoons freshly ground black pepper, 1½ teaspoons ground cloves, 1½ teaspoons ground cumin, 1½ teaspoons ground nutmeg.

• *Pictured page 173*

Sambousek (Lamb and pine nut pastries)

There's always a platter of crispy, golden sambousek on the table when the Saliba family gathers. 'Sambousek has always been my absolute favourite mezze dish,' Reanne says. 'I would sneak into the kitchen as a little girl and Taitare would hand me one, pinch my cheeks and say, "Good girl, my hubibta." She was the most beautiful, gentle woman, and food was her way of showing her love for us all. I hope this recipe can bring you that same warm feeling of a grandmother's love that it brings us.'

Prep time 30–40 mins, plus resting
Cook time 40 mins
Makes approx. 20

2 Tbsp ghee or olive oil
½ brown onion, finely diced
1 garlic clove, finely chopped
500 g (1 lb 2 oz) minced (ground) lamb
1 Tbsp Lebanese spice mix (see Note, page 171)
1 tsp salt
1 Tbsp freshly ground black pepper
½ cup (80 g) toasted pine nuts
Approx. 4 cups (1 litre) sunflower oil, for frying

Pastry
3½ cups (525 g) plain (all-purpose) flour, plus extra for dusting
1 tsp salt
1 tsp sugar
½ cup (125 ml) olive oil
1 cup (250 ml) lukewarm water

For the pastry, use a stand mixer fitted with the paddle attachment to mix together all of the dry ingredients, then add the oil and water and knead on high speed for about 3 minutes. Keep mixing until the dough is no longer sticky and has a slightly oily texture. You can also do this by hand in a large bowl. Tip the dough out onto a benchtop and knead for about 5 minutes. Cover the dough with a tea towel and leave at room temperature for an hour.

For the filling, heat the ghee or oil in a deep frying pan over medium heat. Add the onion and cook, stirring often, for about 10 minutes. Add the garlic and cook, stirring for a few more minutes. Push the onion and garlic to the side of the pan, increase the heat to high and add the lamb mince, pressing it down so that it becomes one large patty with as much of the meat touching the surface of the pan as possible to get the mince thoroughly brown. Cook for a minute or two, then flip over and brown the other side.

Add the spices, salt and pepper and stir into the meat with the onion mixture. Reduce the heat back to medium and cook for about 10 minutes, stirring to break up any clumps of meat. Add the pine nuts, drain any excess liquid and set aside.

Now back to the dough. Cut the dough into four equal pieces and cover three of them again with the tea towel. Working one piece at a time, roll out the dough on a lightly floured benchtop into a 2 mm (¹⁄₁₆ inch) thick circle. Cut out into 10 cm (4 inch) rounds. You should get about five or six from this amount of dough. Roll any excess into a ball and rest to re-use later.

Take about 1 teaspoon of the lamb mixture and place on one half of the dough, but not right to the edge. Fold the other half over so you have a semicircle and crimp the edges with your fingers or the tines of a fork to create a seal. Place on a tray lined with baking paper. Repeat with the remaining dough and lamb mix. Be gentle with the dough – it might feel a bit sticky but it should work with you if you go slowly.

Cover your tray of sambousek and refrigerate until ready to fry.

Heat the sunflower oil in a large saucepan over high heat. Test if it's ready by throwing in a small cube of bread. If it rises to the top and starts frying straight away, the oil is hot enough. Fry the sambousek

Clockwise from top left: Fattoush (page 175); Lamb koftas (page 171); Sambousek

in batches until golden on all sides, about 2–3 minutes each. Remove with a slotted spoon and place on a wire rack to drain. Serve straight away or chill and reheat in the oven, or have cold.

Travel advice

If you're not travelling too far, line a bowl or wide-mouthed thermos with a tea towel or paper towel and fill with the warm sambousek. Tuck the tea towel edges in over the top. Don't put them hot in a container with a sealed lid, as this might create condensation and the pastries will go soggy. If you are transporting them cold, make sure they've fully cooled before packing in an airtight container lined with paper towel. Keep in an insulated ice box or cooler. If you can reheat on arrival, place in a 200°C (400°F) oven for about 15 minutes before serving.

Fattoush (Bread salad)

A good fattoush recipe, with its crunch, colour, big flavour and general joyful deliciousness, is a precious thing. And thanks to Reanne, we can all now claim to have one in our repertoire. I have made this so many times since she shared it with me for this book, it's our current favourite picnic salad and might be yours soon, too!

Prep time 10 mins
Cook time 5 mins
Serves 6–8 as a side dish

2 large pita bread rounds
3 Lebanese (short) cucumbers, halved lengthways and thinly sliced
6 radishes, trimmed and thinly sliced
4 tomatoes, chopped
½ iceberg lettuce, torn into small-ish pieces
10 spring onions (scallions), finely sliced
1 cup (20 g) flat-leaf parsley leaves, roughly chopped
1 cup (20 g) mint leaves, roughly chopped

Dressing
½ tsp Lebanese spice mix (see Note, page 171)
2 tsp ground sumac
1 tsp salt
½ tsp ground black pepper
⅓ cup (80 ml) olive oil
Juice of 1 lemon

Preheat the oven to 180°C (350°F). Tear the pita bread into small pieces and arrange on a large baking tray. Bake for a few minutes or until slightly golden and crunchy. Leave to cool.

Meanwhile, make the dressing by combining all the ingredients in a jug or jar and mixing well. Check the flavour and adjust to taste, then set aside.

Combine all the salad ingredients in a large bowl, add the crisp pita and dressing and toss together gently with your hands.

Travel advice
Make up and transport the salad, pita bread and dressing separately, then combine just before you want to share, otherwise the pita bread may go soggy.

Roasted pumpkin wedges

1. Preheat the oven to 200°C (400°F). Line a couple of baking trays with baking paper.
2. Halve a 2 kg (4 lb 8 oz) Jap pumpkin (squash), remove the seeds and cut into 2–3 cm (¾–1¼ inch) wedges – don't worry about peeling.
3. Drizzle with olive oil and 2 tablespoons Lebanese spice mix (see Note, page 171).
4. Roast for 30 minutes, or until tender.
5. Sprinkle with toasted pepitas (pumpkin seeds) and pine nuts.

Travel advice
Transport cold in an airtight container then reheat on arrival, adding the pepitas and pine nuts at the last minute to prevent softening.

Winter.

Big warm feasts to share, a mid-winter potluck menu, soups for chilly picnics and sturdy loaf cakes for the tin. Here are some of my favourite things to share in the winter sun or around a bonfire in the paddock on a bright cold Sunday.

Soups for the thermos

I have quite the thermos collection. Big ones to keep soup warm for lots of people, medium ones for family 'working picnics' when it's just us four out collecting firewood or doing farm jobs, and baby ones for the kids to take to school. Throughout winter they are used to transport soup to bonfire picnics, and in summer they find themselves storing cold soups (see page 114) or the contents of an icy cold bottle of rosé for a hot evening picnic. But I digress.

Next time you're invited to bring a dish to a wintry gathering, why not pack up one from the following pages, throw in a few mugs, some spoons and bread to dip? Happy days.

There's something a bit special about being passed a steaming mug of soup, with everyone standing around, sipping and dipping and feeling nourished and warmed from the belly out.

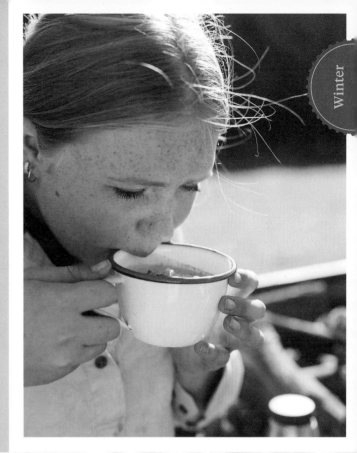

Smooth corn soup with chilli lime crisp

This simple corn soup is comforting, light and zingy - just what you need on a cool winter's day out in the park or paddock. I love, love, love the chilli lime crisp and always make a double batch to have on hand for all kinds of situations (think scrambled eggs, stir-fried greens - that kind of thing).

Prep time 20 mins
Cook time 50 mins
Serves 4-6

4 ears of corn, kernels cut off
2 Tbsp olive oil
1 small brown onion, roughly chopped
2 garlic cloves, roughly chopped
4 cm (1½ inch) piece ginger, roughly chopped

Chilli lime crisp
6 garlic cloves, very finely chopped
4 cm (1½ inch) piece ginger, very finely chopped
1 cup (250 ml) vegetable oil (I use canola)
¼ cup (40 g) toasted sesame seeds
2 star anise
1 cinnamon stick
3 Tbsp sambal oelek
Zest and juice of 2 limes, plus extra lime juice to serve
¼ cup (20 g) fried shallots (available from an Asian grocer)

Place the corn kernels in a bowl, then take the stripped cobs and place these in a large saucepan with 4 cups (1 litre) salted water. Bring to the boil, then simmer for at least 15 minutes but up to 30 minutes. Congratulations, you've just made a super-fast corn stock! Reduce the heat to low and keep warm while you prepare the soup.

For the soup, heat the olive oil in a large saucepan with a lid and add the onion, garlic and ginger. Cook for 5 minutes over low heat or until the garlic is soft and translucent. Add the corn kernels, cover and cook for 5-8 minutes or until the corn has softened. Drain and discard the corn cobs and reserve the stock.

Meanwhile, start making the chilli lime crisp. To do this, place the garlic and ginger in a small saucepan with the vegetable oil. Set the pan over medium heat and bring to a simmer. While the garlic mixture is simmering, combine the sesame seeds, star anise, cinnamon, sambal oelek, lime zest and juice and fried shallots in a ceramic bowl. Pour the hot garlic oil over the spices and stir to combine, then set aside.

To finish the soup, transfer the corn and onion mixture to your blender, pour in 1½ cups (375 ml) of the corn stock (or more, depending on how thin you like your soup) and blitz until velvety smooth. Divide between warm bowls, spoon the chilli lime crisp over the top and add a squeeze of lime juice to taste. Enjoy piping hot in the bright winter sunshine. Yum.

Travel advice
Transport the soup in a thermos or insulated carrier and keep the chilli lime crisp and lime juice separate in an airtight jar to spoon over on serving.

Spiced vegetable, lemon and lentil soup

This soup is a staple in our house during winter. It's dahl-ish in texture and, in fact, you could easily reduce the liquid content and have it as a dahl if you prefer. I adore it for weekday work lunches and picnics alike with a dollop of plain yoghurt, some flatbreads and a lime pickle, finely chopped kimchi or a squeeze of lime for tang.

Prep time 10 mins
Cook time 50 mins
Serves 6–8

2 Tbsp vegetable or coconut oil
2 brown onions, finely diced
½ tsp chilli flakes, plus extra
  to serve
1 Tbsp cumin seeds
1 Tbsp yellow mustard seeds
½ tsp coriander seeds
1 tsp ground coriander
6 green cardamom pods, bruised
4 carrots, finely chopped
2 celery stalks, finely chopped
200 g (7 oz) red lentils, well
  rinsed and drained
400 ml (14 fl oz) tin coconut milk
3 cups (750 ml) chicken stock
400 g (14 oz) tin cherry tomatoes
3 Tbsp tomato paste
  (concentrated purée)
Juice of 2 lemons
2 handfuls baby spinach
1 handful coriander (cilantro)
  leaves, finely chopped
  (optional)

Heat the oil in a large saucepan over medium heat. Add the onion and cook for 10 minutes, or until soft and translucent. Add the chilli, cumin, mustard seeds, coriander and cardamom and cook for a further few minutes, or until everything is soft and aromatic.

Add the carrot and celery and cook, stirring often, for 5 minutes.

Next, add the lentils, coconut milk, stock, tomatoes, tomato paste and lemon juice and stir well. Reduce the heat and simmer for 30 minutes, or until the lentils are tender.

Check the flavour, add some salt if you think it needs it, then stir through the spinach just before serving hot with a sprinkling of coriander and extra chilli, if using.

Travel advice
Pack your soup nice and hot in a thermos then fill and pack a few little jars with yoghurt, pickle, chilli flakes – whatever you fancy. I have a cupboard just for enamel cups, jars and picnic things, which makes it easy to grab and go!

Pear and parsnip soup

The mellow flavours of this soup are always a favourite in my family. It's great in little mugs as a starter, or in a bigger mug or bowl as a main, perhaps with batons of crunchy toasted Turkish bread, a sprinkle of toasted walnuts and a few nigella seeds. I love the flavour of toasted fennel seeds in this recipe, but if you want a really nice, simple soup, just leave them out.

Prep time 15 mins
Cook time 40 mins
Serves 6–8 as a starter, 4 as a
  main

25 g (1 oz) butter
2 leeks, washed and finely
  chopped
2 ripe Beurre Bosc pears, peeled
  and roughly chopped (or you
  could use green apples)
6 parsnips, peeled and roughly
  chopped
½ tsp toasted fennel seeds
  (optional)
3 cups (750 ml) chicken stock
½ cup (125 ml) thick (double)
  cream
toasted walnuts or hazelnuts and
  a drizzle of walnut oil, to serve

Melt the butter in a large saucepan over medium heat and add the leek. Cook, stirring often, for about 10 minutes, or until completely soft.

Add the pear, parsnip and the fennel seeds, if using, and cook for a couple more minutes, stirring as you go. Pour in the stock, reduce the heat to a simmer and cook for 25 minutes, or until the parsnips are completely tender. Pour into a blender and blitz until smooth, stir in the cream and season just before serving. Scatter with toasted walnuts and a drizzle of walnut oil to serve.

Travel advice
Keep hot in a thermos and pack the nuts and oil separately. Pour, drizzle and sip on arrival!

Dippy and nibbly things

'Just bring nibbles': three words that can freeze anyone up. Being asked to bring nibbles could be seen as the 'dud' assignment, a cue to go to the shops and drop $60 on cheese, crackers and containers of dip that you then have to try to make look half decent on arrival. Not anymore! Instead, let's try these fun, fancy dip ideas that will bring the flavour, look great, disappear in minutes and have everyone asking for the recipe.

Dill pickle and salmon dip

I'll take pickles with, and in, anything, so this dip is my favourite! I love it with salt and vinegar chips.

Prep time 5 mins
Cook time NIL
Serves 8

1 cup (140 g) dill pickles, roughly chopped
¼ cup (65 g) sour cream
½ cup (130 g) plain yoghurt
150 g (5½ oz) hot-smoked salmon, flaked
1 garlic clove, finely grated
Zest of 1 small lemon
1 small handful dill leaves, chopped

Stir everything together well and season to taste.

Carrot top pesto

Serve as a dip or bundle up in a jar with a packet of nice pasta, a hunk of cheese and a bottle of wine. Give it to a friend and make their day.

Prep time 10 mins
Cook time NIL
Makes about 1½ cups (450 g)

2 cups (120 g) carrot tops, washed
    and roughly chopped
2 cups (100 g) basil leaves
⅔ cup (100 g) pine nuts, toasted
Zest and juice of 1 lemon, plus extra if needed
75 g (2¾ oz) freshly grated parmesan
½ cup (125 ml) extra virgin olive oil

Combine all the ingredients in a food processor with some salt and pepper and blitz to a rough paste. Adjust the flavour with more lemon or salt if needed.

Travel advice
Store dips in airtight containers and keep chilled until about 20 minutes before serving so they're not 'fridge cold'.

From top: Dill pickle and salmon dip; Carrot top pesto; Roasted carrot hummus with quick pickles and pita (page 188)

Roasted carrot hummus
with quick pickles and pita

This is something I turn to time and time again; it's healthy, super tasty and a nice change from your usual dip offering. It's also perfect with beetroot instead of carrot, and as you can imagine, yields a beautiful colour. To make toasted pita bread triangles, follow the recipe on page 117 for the pita cups, but cut the bread into triangles instead. Brush with olive oil, sprinkle with sesame seeds and a little sea salt, then pop in the oven till golden.

Prep time 10 mins
Cook time 50 mins
Serves 6–8

4 carrots, trimmed, peeled
  and roughly chopped
4 garlic cloves, unpeeled
1 small brown onion, cut
  into eighths
1 tsp cumin seeds
⅓ cup (80 ml) olive oil
1 tsp sea salt
400 g (14 oz) tin chickpeas,
  drained and rinsed
1 heaped Tbsp tahini
Juice of 1 lemon
⅓ cup (40 g) walnuts, toasted
  and roughly chopped
Pomegranate molasses,
  for drizzling
Toasted pita bread triangles
  (see above) and Quick pickles
  (see below), to serve

Preheat the oven to 180°C (350°F). Place the carrot, garlic, onion and cumin seeds in a roasting tin and drizzle with half the olive oil. Sprinkle in the sea salt and toss well to combine.

Roast for 30 minutes, or until the carrots are soft. Tip in the chickpeas, toss everything around again and return to the oven for another 20 minutes, or until the carrots are beginning to caramelise and the chickpeas take on some colour.

Remove from the oven. At this point, you could serve the carrots and chickpeas on a bed of labne (see page 170) with some baby spinach as a delicious salad or proceed to the dip stage…

Tip the contents of the roasting tin into a blender or food processor. Add the tahini, lemon juice and remaining olive oil and blend until smooth. Add ⅓ cup (80 ml) water as you go until you are happy with the consistency.

Season to taste, and check if the hummus needs a little more lemon juice. To serve, sprinkle with the walnuts and drizzle with the molasses. Pop on a platter with the toasted pita bread and quick pickles.

Travel advice
Store the hummus in an airtight container and keep chilled until about 20 minutes before serving so it's not 'fridge cold'.

Quick pickles

1. Follow the method for pickled beetroot on page 118, but substitute in a bunch of washed, trimmed and peeled baby carrots. You could do the same with sliced radishes, too.
2. Pack the vegetables into jars and pour in the pickling liquid to cover (you might need to press or weigh down the vegetables to keep them submerged).
3. Leave to cool in the fridge for at least an hour before using. They'll keep in the fridge for a couple of weeks.

Travel advice
Transport straight from the fridge in a tightly sealed glass jar.

• *Pictured page 186*

Warm caramelised onion dip
with baguette croutons

There's no pretending that this is a healthy treat. But it is a treat (is it ever). It's also quite rich and filling, so a little goes a long way. As well as the croutons, you could serve this golden bubbling dip with a tray of crunchy raw vegetables, such as fennel, carrot and celery sticks.

Prep time 20 mins
Cook time 1 hour 10 mins
Serves 6

⅓ cup (80 ml) olive oil
4 large brown onions, thinly
  sliced
2 Tbsp thyme leaves, plus extra
  to sprinkle
¼ cup (60 ml) apple cider
  vinegar
1 Tbsp Worcestershire sauce
1 tsp sea salt
250 g (9 oz) cream cheese
¾ cup (185 g) sour cream
1 cup (100 g) grated mild cheese
½ cup (50 g) grated parmesan
1 cup (60 g) coarse breadcrumbs
1 baguette

Heat 2 tablespoons of the olive oil in a large frying pan over medium heat and add the onion, cooking until darkly caramelised and very soft, at least 30 minutes. At the end of the cooking time, stir in the thyme leaves, apple cider vinegar, Worcestershire sauce, the sea salt and plenty of ground black pepper.

Set the onions aside to cool a smidge, then transfer to a gratin or any shallow 2–3 cup (500–750 ml) capacity ovenproof dish.

In a mixing bowl, combine the cream cheese, sour cream and grated cheese and stir well.

Preheat the oven to 180°C (350°F).

Spoon the cream cheese mixture on top of the onions, sprinkle with the breadcrumbs and place in the oven for 30 minutes, or until brown and beginning to bubble. If you feel it needs extra colour on top, pop it under a hot grill (broiler) right at the end.

Cut the baguette into fairly thin slices and arrange on a baking tray lined with baking paper. Brush or rub with the remaining olive oil and sprinkle with some salt and pepper to taste. Toast in the preheated oven for about 10 minutes on each side, or until golden brown. Once completely cool, these will keep well (in an airtight container) for 1 week.

<u>Travel advice</u>
This recipe really needs to be served hot or warm for maximum flavour, so if taking it to a party, make sure you can pop it in an oven when you get there. Just transport it in the ovenproof dish in a cooler bag or ice box. Or, if you're taking this to a picnic where there's a barbecue or hotplate, cook it all as per the above but transport it in a dish that can go over heat and warm up from the bottom beforehand.

• Pictured page 191

From left: Roasted
carrot hummus with
quick pickles and
pita (page 188); Dill
pickle and salmon dip
(page 187); Carrot top
pesto (page 187);
Warm caramelised
onion dip with baguette
croutons (page 189)

Outdoor lunch on a cold day

A cold day out in the bright winter sun, a table heaped with glazed ham, tender beef ribs, roast veggies, garlic bread, pickles and cakes, then Irish coffee for dessert. How good does that sound?

Let's make it all (or some, and delegate the rest), get a group together, rug up and head outside this weekend for a winter feast inspired by these two wonderful cooks: Ree Booth and Sophie Comiskey. Both live near Oberon, New South Wales, not too far from me and are all about using the best produce they can (usually home-grown) and cooking simply and seasonally.

Winter picnics are my favourite - no snakes, flies or blistering heat to spoil our food. And we can safely light a fire for warmth. Add some bright sunshine, Wedgewood-blue skies and a table of tasty food to share, all while rugged up on a hillside, and I'm in heaven.

Braised beef short ribs

This is Ree's recipe, and it's an absolute winner. I have made it many times since she shared it, always with great success. It's easy to bring together, it tastes wonderful and is a main dish of substance - a great thing to take to any gathering.

Prep time 20 mins, plus
  marinating
Cook time 4–6 hours
Serves 6–8

1.2 kg (2 lb 12 oz) beef short ribs
2 handfuls green beans, trimmed

Marinade
3 Tbsp olive oil
1 Tbsp chopped fresh thyme
  leaves
2 garlic cloves, crushed
1 Tbsp smoked paprika
½ tsp cayenne pepper
1 Tbsp salt
1 tsp ground black pepper

Cooking sauce
1 Tbsp olive oil
1 brown onion, diced
1 heaped Tbsp tomato paste
  (concentrated purée)
⅓ cup (80 ml) Worcestershire
  sauce
2 cups (500 ml) chicken stock

Trim the ribs of any excess fat and place them in a large container. Combine the marinade ingredients in a small bowl, add to the ribs and mix and rub to coat them all well. Cover and place in the fridge to marinate overnight, or for at least 4–6 hours.

Heat the barbecue or a hotplate to high and sear the ribs on all sides until they are nicely browned. Set aside while you make the cooking sauce.

Preheat the oven to 140°C (275°F).

Heat the oil in a large casserole dish over medium heat and cook the onion for about 10 minutes, or until soft and translucent. Add the tomato paste, Worcestershire sauce and stock and bring to a simmer. Reduce the heat and add the beef ribs. Transfer to the oven and cook slowly for 4–6 hours, or until the meat is tender and almost falling off the bone. Add the green beans for the last 10 minutes of cooking time. Serve warm.

Travel advice
Try to time the cooking so the ribs will be done just before heading out the door. They should keep their heat for a while, but if you have access to a hotplate or oven, perhaps give them a quick reheat just before serving. To help with this, wrap the casserole dish in a couple of tea towels and ensure the lid is securely tied down, then tuck into a laundry basket with some towels to keep as much heat in as possible.

Orange and honey glazed ham

Why do we forget about glazed ham unless it's Christmas or 2am after a wedding? A whole, gloriously glazed leg is such a fantastic way to feed a big group, and almost everyone delights at the sight of a spread of glazed ham, bread, mustards and pickles. And yes, I realise they're not super cheap, but one ham feeds a lot of people, so you do get bang for your buck. This glaze is Sophie Comiskey's (thank you), and the ham comes from her farm near Oberon, New South Wales. They cure the meat themselves and it honestly is the best I've ever had.

Prep time 20 mins
Cook time 1 hour
Serves 6–8

4–6 kg (8 lb 12 oz–13 lb 3½ oz) whole ham leg
Small handful of whole cloves

Glaze
1 cup (250 ml) orange juice
1 cup (350 g) honey
2 garlic cloves, crushed
4 star anise
2 Tbsp dijon mustard
3 oranges, thinly sliced

Preheat the oven to 180°C (350°F).

Use a sharp knife to cut around the ham leg, running the knife under the skin and right around the edge of the ham. Gently pull the skin back in one piece, using your fingers to push between the rind and fat. Reserve the skin for storing the ham.

Score the fat in a diamond pattern and stud each point with a single clove. Cover the exposed bone in foil.

Mix the glaze ingredients together in a large jug.

Grab the biggest roasting tin you have and pour in water to come 1–2 cm (½–¾ inches) up the side. Put a wire rack in the tin, pop the ham on top and brush with one-third of the glaze. Pick the orange slices out of the glaze and arrange them on top of the ham, securing them with toothpicks. Roast for 1 hour, pulling the ham out every 20 minutes to baste with more of the glaze and top up the water if needed.

Serve warm or at room temperature.

Travel advice
This ham is wonderful both straight from the oven and at room temperature. If it's hot, slice what you need right on serving, then wrap the ham in foil and store in an insulated ice box or cooler until you need to replenish!

Note
Cooked ham must be stored in the fridge or an insulated ice box or cooler. Cover with the skin you peeled off earlier, then place in a fabric bag soaked in a vinegar solution. To make the solution, add a good splash of vinegar to a sink that you have filled about halfway with water, dunk the bag in and give it a good hand wash. An old pillowcase works well. Rinse and re-soak the ham bag in vinegar solution every 3 days. Keep the ham for up to a week, but use your nose, too; if it starts to smell dodgy, it probably is!

The sides

Sides are my favourite thing to bring to a picnic or gathering like this, mostly because the stakes aren't at all high. It's not like we're tasked with bringing the main event for everyone; the pressure is off and we can get a bit more creative and stretch the brief a little. Thank you so much to Sophie and Ree for sharing this fantastic selection of wintry sides.

GARLIC BREAD

Preheat the oven to 180°C (350°F). Finely chop 6 garlic cloves and stir through 150 g (5½ oz) soft unsalted butter. Slice a large sourdough loaf almost all the way through and spread each 'slice' with a good smear of garlic butter. Season with salt and pepper. Wrap the loaf in foil and bake for 30 minutes, then tear or cut open the foil to expose the top of the bread, sprinkle with a little grated parmesan and return to the oven for a final 20 minutes.

Travel advice

Wrap in foil and a couple of tea towels to keep warm.

ROASTED PUMPKIN WITH DUKKAH

Slice your pumpkin (squash) into wedges (peel the skin off or leave it on as Ree did – see opposite). Place on a baking tray, drizzle with olive oil and season with salt and pepper. Roast at 160°C (315°F) for 1 hour, or until completely soft and beginning to caramelise around the edges. Transfer to a serving platter, crumble some goat's cheese or feta on top, sprinkle generously with dukkah (see page 113) or roasted roughly chopped almonds, and finish with a drizzle of pomegranate molasses and a squeeze of lemon.

Travel advice

As soon as the pumpkin comes out of the oven, cover with foil and wrap in a tea towel to keep some heat in. Sprinkle with the toppings right before serving.

BRUSSELS SPROUTS WITH BACON

This is as good at room temperature as it is straight out of the pan, so it's another one of those handy dishes you can take to a party and know it will still be good after a couple of hours. (Thank you, Ree, for this recipe inspiration!) Chop about 300 g (10½ oz) bacon into lardons and fry in a splash of olive oil in a deep, heavy-based frying pan until crispy. Remove the bacon, set the pan over low heat and add 3 finely chopped garlic cloves. Cook until just aromatic, then add 500 g (1 lb 2 oz) halved and trimmed brussels sprouts. Increase the heat and cook for 5 minutes or until the sprouts have softened and turned bright green. Return the bacon to the pan, add the juice of 1 lemon and season well with salt and pepper.

Travel advice

Cover with foil and wrap in a tea towel to keep warm.

BOILED EGGS WITH BACON

A simple but delicious addition to any picnic or feast. Just hard-boil and peel eggs, then halve and arrange on a nice plate with some strips of crisp bacon, good mayonnaise for dolloping, some chopped chives and freshly ground pepper. Sprinkle with sea salt to taste.

Travel advice

If travelling far, peel the eggs on arrival and assemble right before serving. Otherwise, do it all at home and keep chilled while en route.

ROASTED GARLIC POTATOES

Place enough potatoes for your crew in a large casserole dish or deep roasting tin. Dot with about 20 g (¾ oz) butter per potato, season with salt and pepper, and add a head of garlic, sliced in half horizontally. Roast in a hot oven (200°C/400°F) for about 1 hour or until the potatoes are tender when pierced with a knife. About halfway through cooking, toss everything around so the butter coats the potatoes evenly.

Travel advice

Transport these in the casserole dish or roasting tin, wrapped tightly with foil and a couple of tea towels. If you have access to a barbecue, perhaps tip them onto the hotplate to fry up a little.

Tips for a wintry outdoor lunch

They say there's no such thing as bad weather, only unsuitable clothes. I feel the same about picnics: with the right gear and food, any day can be a good one for an outing. And any meal can make a good picnic, whether it's in a paddock or your back garden – just do it! Here are some more ideas:

- Try any of the soups on pages 180–4 packed in a thermos, plus some buttered bread rolls for dipping.
- For dessert, bake The easiest cake in the world (page 222) in a slice tin (see page 48) and cut it into squares. Serve with sharp cheddar and tart apple.

- Invest in some picnic 'kit': enamel cups, plates, a thermos, picnic basket, etc, and keep it all together somewhere handy so you can grab and go.
- Organise your friends for a Friday afternoon walk or hike, pack a backpack with sliced focaccia (see pages 94–5) and pour a bottle of cold wine into a thermos, then head out for an 'end of the week' drinks party, al fresco.
- If it's really cold, maybe bake a potato per person to keep in their pocket as a hand-warmer, then later slice into it and fill with butter (ideally the Miso butter on page 137) and cheese for an excellent snack.
- *Ree and her crew are extra committed to good coffee on their picnics, so much so that they bring a generator and a coffee machine!*

Almond and lime syrup cake

Thank you, Ree, for sharing this recipe. This is a super moist gluten-free cake and, with all that lime, it's light and zingy and a great way to end a big meal.

Prep time 15 mins
Cook time 1 hour
Serves 8

2 cups (200 g) almond meal
⅔ cup (100 g) gluten-free flour
    (see Note)
1 cup (90 g) desiccated coconut
1 tsp gluten-free baking powder
    (see Note)
Zest of 2 limes, juice reserved
1 cup (250 g) salted butter,
    melted, plus extra for greasing
2 eggs, separated
1 cup (250 ml) full-cream milk
250 g (9 oz) caster (superfine)
    sugar

Syrup
100 g (3½ oz) caster (superfine)
    sugar
Zest and juice of 3 limes
½ cup (125 ml) pure maple
    syrup, or honey

Preheat the oven to 180°C (350°F) and grease and line a 20 cm (8 inch) cake tin.

Combine the almond meal, flour, coconut, baking powder and lime zest in a large bowl. Stir in the melted butter. Place the egg yolks in a small bowl and whisk in the milk. Fold this into the flour mixture until you have a smooth batter.

In a separate bowl, whisk the egg whites and sugar to stiff peaks. Fold this through the cake batter, then transfer to the cake tin. Bake for 1 hour, or until a skewer inserted in the middle of the cake comes out clean.

Make the syrup in the last 10 minutes of the cake's cooking time. Combine the sugar and 150 ml (5 fl oz) water in a small saucepan over medium heat and stir until the sugar dissolves. Add the lime zest and juice, along with the juice from the two limes we zested earlier for the cake. Bring to a gentle boil, then reduce the heat and add the maple syrup. Simmer for about 5 minutes, then remove from the heat and set aside.

Remove the cake from the oven and gently poke holes in the top with a fork. Slowly pour the syrup over the cake and allow it to soak in before serving.

Serve with thick (double) cream in winter or ice cream and fruit salad in summer.

Travel advice
This can be made and transported in the baking tin, syrup and all. But if you have a barbecue or hotplate on site, pack the syrup separately, bring to boiling point in a little saucepan and pour it over the cake right before serving – such a treat.

Note
You can swap the gluten-free flour for plain (all-purpose) flour and use regular baking powder, if preferred.

Irish coffee mix

I can't think of many nicer ways to finish a wintry feast outside than with a small mug of this Irish coffee and perhaps some good marshmallows. It is Just. So. Good. Thank you, Ree, for the idea and recipe.

Prep time 5 mins
Cook time 5 mins
Makes approx. 2½ cups (625 ml)

½ cup (125 ml) Dubliner (honey-flavoured Irish whisky), or your favourite whisky with honey or maple syrup, to taste
1 heaped Tbsp cacao powder
300 ml (10½ fl oz) single (pure) cream
200 g (7 oz) dulce de leche or condensed milk
1 tsp vanilla extract
1 cup (250 ml) espresso coffee

Place all the ingredients, except the coffee, in a blender and blitz on medium speed for 30 seconds or until fully combined and lightly thickened. Warm in a small saucepan and transfer to a pre-warmed thermos. Pour the hot coffee into another pre-warmed thermos and invite your lucky friends to make their own Irish coffee.

Travel advice
Transport the warm whiskey mixture and coffee in pre-warmed thermoses.

Notes
• *I'm inspired to follow Ree's lead and bring a generator and a coffee machine to my picnics. I'll get there one day, but in the meantime a thermos will have to do!*
• *For a summer version, replace the hot coffee with ¼ cup (60 ml) cooled espresso coffee and serve over ice.*
• *A bottle of whisky mixer makes a great Christmas gift, too.*

Meringue-topped chocolate cake

Okay, so you might think, red kidney beans in a cake? Not so much. But bear with me because this wonderful cake is so deeply flavoured and moist, but also the kind that feels a bit healthy, too. Bonus! I recommend making the meringue in advance as it does hog the oven for quite a while and can be stored in an airtight container for up to a week. Huge thank you to Sophie Comiskey for sharing this really excellent recipe.

Prep time 25 mins, plus cooling
Cook time 2 hours 10 mins
Serves 8–10

400 g (14 oz) tin red kidney beans, drained and rinsed
1 Tbsp strong brewed instant or espresso coffee
5 eggs
1 tsp natural vanilla extract
120 g (4¼ oz) unsalted butter, plus extra for greasing
70 ml (2¼ fl oz) coconut oil
120 g (4¼ oz) cooking chocolate
140 g (5 oz) rapadura (unrefined) sugar
70 g (2½ oz) cacao powder
1 tsp baking powder
½ tsp bicarbonate of soda (baking soda)
¼ tsp sea salt
½ cup (165 g) apricot jam, or whatever you prefer

Meringue
150 ml (5 fl oz) egg whites
1 cup (220 g) caster (superfine) sugar
1 Tbsp cornflour (cornstarch), sifted
1 tsp white vinegar

Preheat the oven to 200°C (400°F) and line the base of a 20 cm (8 inch) springform cake tin with baking paper.

To make the meringue, beat the egg whites to stiff peaks. Add the caster sugar, one spoonful at a time, until it is all incorporated and the mixture is glossy. Add the cornflour and vinegar and beat for 5 seconds.

Transfer the mixture to your tin and use a spatula to bring the top together to form a dome.

Just before putting the meringue in the oven, reduce the heat to 100°C (200°F) and let a little of the heat out by opening the oven door for a few seconds. Cook for 1½ hours, and don't be tempted to open the oven door at any time. Once cooked, turn off the oven and leave the meringue inside to cool for a further hour before removing. Remove from the cake tin and place on a wire rack to cool.

Preheat the oven to 180°C (350°F) and grease and line a 20 cm (8 inch) cake tin.

Combine the kidney beans, coffee, eggs and vanilla in a food processor or blender and blitz to a smooth, thick consistency.

Place the butter, oil and chocolate in a saucepan over low heat and cook, stirring as you go, until everything is melted and well combined into a glossy mixture.

Add the rapadura sugar, cacao powder, baking powder, bicarbonate of soda and salt to the food processor and pulse until just combined. Add the chocolate and butter mixture, too, and give it a blitz for a few seconds to combine. Transfer the mixture to the tin and bake for 40 minutes, or until the top of the cake feels firm and a skewer inserted in the middle comes out clean.

Remove from the oven and allow to cool on a wire rack.

Brush the cooled cake with the jam (it will act as a sort of glue) and place the meringue on top.

Travel advice
This one travels pretty well, but if going any big distance I'd keep the meringue 'hat' separate, wrapped tightly in foil and sealed in an airtight container, then pop it on the cake just before serving.

Sturdy cakes

Sometimes a sturdy cake is in order – one that will travel well and won't drip or spoil or topple in the car. A cake that sits in its container or tin quite happily, even for days, ready and waiting for coffee, tea or dessert as needed.

At times like these I make this lovely almond loaf cake, with twists, turns and additions according to the season, mood and preferences of its intended recipient (there are two of my favourite variations on page 210). In fact, I turn to this base recipe so often that I have the quantities on a sticky note on the fridge, ready to go whenever needed.

Orange and rosemary almond loaf (page 210)

Almond loaf

This is a classic butter cake formula with almond meal for extra flavour and moisture. It's delicious as is, or you can use it as the base for an orange and rosemary loaf (pictured here) or a double chocolate loaf - see recipes on page 210.

Prep time 25 mins
Cook time 45–60 mins
Serves 8

1 cup (250 g) unsalted butter, at room temperature, plus extra for greasing
250 g (9 oz) caster (superfine) sugar
4 eggs, at room temperature
200 g (1⅓ cups) plain (all-purpose) flour
1 cup (100 g) almond meal
2 tsp baking powder
A pinch of salt
½ cup (125 ml) buttermilk
1 tsp vanilla paste

Preheat the oven to 180°C (350°F) and grease and line a large 30 × 15 cm (12 × 6 inch) loaf tin.
　Combine the butter and sugar in the bowl of a stand mixer fitted with the paddle attachment, or use a large bowl and an electric mixer, and beat until pale and fluffy. Add the eggs, one at a time, beating well between each addition (stop and scrape down the side of the bowl every now and then if needed).
　Place the flour, almond meal, baking powder and salt in a small bowl and whisk to combine. Place the buttermilk in a separate bowl and whisk in the vanilla.
　Fold half the buttermilk and half the flour mixture into the butter mix, then repeat with the remaining buttermilk and flour. If your mixer has a large whisk attachment, use this, but do it by hand. Otherwise, use a regular spatula.
　Transfer the mixture to your tin and bake for 45–50 minutes, or until a skewer inserted in the middle of the cake comes out clean.

Travel advice
Let the cake cool completely, then wrap tightly in foil or store in an airtight container.

Variations

ORANGE AND ROSEMARY ALMOND LOAF

Begin the recipe as on page 209, but before adding the butter to your mixer, grate in the zest of 2 oranges and add the finely chopped leaves of 1 rosemary sprig to the sugar and rub it in well with your fingers to really infuse the orange and rosemary flavours. Fish out as many of the rosemary leaves as you can (it's fine to leave one or two in there).

Continue with the base recipe.

While the cake is cooking, thinly slice the oranges you zested earlier and place in a small saucepan with 2 rosemary sprigs, 100 g (3½ oz) caster (superfine) sugar, 1 teaspoon vanilla paste and 300 ml (10½ fl oz) water. Stir to combine and cook over low heat for about 20 minutes or until the oranges have completely softened.

As soon as the cake comes out of the oven, spoon the oranges and syrup over it. Enjoy warm with some tangy plain yoghurt.

Travel advice

Because of the syrup here, I'd transport, slice and enjoy straight from the baking tin. It's so much easier and the cake is protected on even the bumpiest of roads!

Note

To convert this into a slice, swap the loaf tin for an 18 x 27 cm (7 x 10¾ inch) tin and reduce the cooking time to 25–35 minutes. Omit the orange slices on top and ice the slice with a simple orange icing. Mix 1 cup (125 g) icing (confectioners') sugar with the grated zest of 1 orange and a little of the juice. Whisk until you have a smooth, fairly thick icing, adding more juice (a very little at a time) until you're happy with the consistency. Pour the icing over the cooled slice and smooth the top.

DOUBLE CHOCOLATE ALMOND LOAF

Before beginning the base recipe from page 209, melt 100 g (3½ oz) dark chocolate (minimum 70% cocoa) in a double-boiler or microwave and set aside.

Proceed with the base recipe, but when whisking the vanilla into the buttermilk, add ½ cup (125 ml) warm (but not hot) strong espresso and the melted chocolate. When combining the dry ingredients, add 30 g (1 oz) good-quality cocoa powder.

Continue with the base recipe but, before you transfer the mixture to the tin, fold in an extra 100 g (3½ oz) roughly chopped dark chocolate.

Travel advice

Let the cake cool completely, then wrap tightly in foil or store in an airtight container.

Note

You can also serve this as a brownie. Swap the loaf tin for an 18 x 27 cm (7 x 10¾ inch) tin and reduce the cooking time to 25–35 minutes. Finish with a dusting of icing (confectioners') sugar.

• Pictured page 209

Windy Station Woolshed in the Liverpool Plains Shire of New South Wales is a huge Federation Carpenter-style structure. Building began on it in 1901. These days it is being lovingly restored and used as an event and gathering space.

Crowd pleasers

Windy Station is home to one of Australia's oldest and biggest woolsheds. In its heyday, in the early 1900s, about 60,000 sheep were shorn here every year and the shed was filled with 100 shearers, shedhands, wool classers, wool pressers and rouseabouts working nonstop.

I can't help thinking about the hard-working shearers' cooks who, decade on decade, would have fed hundreds of hungry people a hot meal three times a day. I guess they had a stash of 'back pocket' recipes to rely on – ones that always worked and that the crew loved.

Country cooks have always been good at this; they all seem to have an arsenal of bomb-proof recipes that everyone loves, dishes that can be made without fuss and with success, every time.

Here are a couple of mine, and one contributed kindly by Clare Lee, the current custodian of this incredibly special shed.

Rice, potato and chorizo pilaf

We all love a one-tray wonder, especially when it takes just a few pantry staples and turns them into a deeply flavoured dish of contrasting textures and moreish flavours. I make this regularly and year-round, tweaking according to the season and whatever I have in the fridge. This is a pretty basic version, so you can really make it your own. Leave out the chorizo, or serve the pilaf as a side dish (or bed) for slow-cooked lamb, pan-fried fish or barbecued chicken. Or swap out the sour cream for a tangy yoghurt and spinach sauce (see page 18).

Prep time 20 mins
Cook time 2 hours
Serves 6–8

2 cups (400 g) brown rice
¼ cup (60 g) butter
4 onions, thinly sliced
3 chorizo sausages, sliced into
  1 cm (½ inch) rounds
1 Tbsp ground cumin
1 Tbsp smoked paprika
1 tsp sea salt
1 tsp freshly ground black pepper
Zest and juice of 1 lemon
3 large potatoes, peeled and
  sliced into thin rounds
4 cups (1 litre) chicken or
  vegetable stock
1 cup (100 g) freshly grated
  parmesan
Sour cream, to serve

Place the rice in a bowl, fill it with cold water and leave it to soak.

Heat the butter in a large, heavy-based frying pan and add the onion. Cook over medium–low heat, stirring regularly, for 30 minutes or until dark brown and deeply caramelised. Remove three-quarters of the onion and set aside.

Increase the heat under your pan to medium–high, add the chorizo, spices, salt, pepper and lemon zest and juice and stir for a couple of minutes. Drain and rinse the rice under cold water, then add it to the pan. Stir and cook for a couple more minutes until every grain is slick and coated with the spiced oil.

Preheat the oven to 180°C (350°F).

Transfer half of the mixture to an ovenproof dish, then top with half of the potatoes in a layer. Add the remaining rice mixture, then the remaining potato slices. Pour in enough stock to cover everything by about 1 cm (½ inch). Top up with water if you think you need a little more. Cover tightly with foil, then bake in the oven for 1 hour or until the rice and potatoes are tender and cooked through. Check after 45 minutes and add more water if it is looking at all dry.

Remove the foil and add the reserved onion and grated parmesan. Increase the heat to 220°C (425°F) and cook for a final 20 minutes, or until golden.

Serve hot from the oven or at room temperature with sour cream to dollop on top.

Travel advice

While this is good at room temperature, it's even better hot. So time things so it comes out of the oven right before heading off then cover tightly with foil, followed by a couple of tea towels. If your cooler is big enough, place some heat packs (or even a hot water bottle) on the bottom, line with newspaper, then pop your wrapped dish on top. That should keep plenty of heat in, for a while at least.

Beef tagine with coconut quinoa

Feeding the masses with little fuss and great generosity seems to be a built-in skill for many country people - case in point, Clare Lee. Windy's current woolshed manager lives on site with her family, and is the woman charged with restoring and keeping this historic building open for events and visitors. She's a wonderful cook and rustles up big, beautiful lunches without breaking a sweat. This tagine is a classic example of the kind of tasty food that Clare whips up. The quinoa is easy to prepare in advance, and makes a nice change from couscous.

Prep time 30 mins, plus
  marinating
Cook time 3 hours 10 mins
Serves 6–8

600 g (1 lb 5 oz) beef chuck,
  cut into 5 cm (2 inch) cubes
¼ cup (60 ml) olive oil
1 onion, chopped
1 bunch coriander (cilantro),
  stalks and leaves separated
400 g (14 oz) tin chopped
  tomatoes
600 ml (21 fl oz) vegetable stock
500 g (1 lb 2 oz) sweet potato,
  peeled and cut into large
  chunks
100 g (3½ oz) pitted prunes
Greek-style yoghurt, to serve

Spice rub
1 Tbsp ras el hanout
1 Tbsp ground cumin
1 Tbsp ground ginger
1 Tbsp sweet paprika
1 tsp ground cinnamon

Coconut quinoa
2 cups (400 g) tri-colour quinoa
2 Tbsp shredded coconut
400 ml (14 fl oz) tin coconut
  cream

Throw all the spice rub ingredients in a bowl with the diced beef and give it a good massage. Cover for a few hours or leave in the fridge overnight.

Meanwhile, if you are using a traditional earthenware tagine, submerge it in some water for a couple of hours so it doesn't crack when heated. A heavy-based Dutch oven or ovenproof saucepan will also work well.

Once you are ready to cook, heat a couple of tablespoons of the oil in the tagine over high heat and brown the beef on all sides. Remove the beef, add more oil if needed and cook the onion and coriander stalks, stirring often, for 10 minutes, or until the onion is translucent.

Return the beef to the pan and add the tomatoes and 400 ml (14 fl oz) of the stock, then stir to combine. Bring to boiling point, then reduce the heat and simmer for 1½ hours.

Add the sweet potato, prunes and the remaining stock. Cover again and cook, this time over the lowest heat on your stovetop, for another 1½ hours. Add a little water to the pot halfway through if you think the tagine is getting a little dry.

After 3 hours or so of slow cooking, the beef and sweet potatoes should be lovely and tender. If you think there is a little too much liquid, leave the lid off for the last 20 minutes of cooking so some of it evaporates.

About 20 minutes before the tagine is ready, prepare the coconut quinoa. Put the quinoa, coconut and coconut cream in a saucepan and stir to combine. Bring to the boil, then reduce the heat to a simmer. Pop the lid on and cook over low heat for 15 minutes, or until the quinoa has fluffed up a little and is lovely and soft.

Serve the tagine with the coriander leaves and a bowl of thick Greek-style yoghurt. Enjoy with the coconut quinoa.

Travel advice
Either transport the hot tagine in an insulated carrier bag, or chill it right down in the fridge, transport in an insulated cooler and reheat on arrival. The quinoa is good cold but better warm, so try transporting it hot in an insulated bowl or thick-sided container wrapped in a towel.

Green curry drumsticks

This is one tasty dish. Bright and bursting with flavour, yet comforting and easy to eat all at the same time. The kind of thing I'd adore either on a summer's picnic or a cold winter's evening. In short, a year-round winner. This is good hot or at room temperature.

Prep time 20 mins, plus marinating
Cook time 1 hour
Serves 6–8

8 chicken drumsticks
olive oil, for browning
400 ml (14 fl oz) tin coconut milk

Marinade
2 tsp ground turmeric
2 garlic cloves, finely chopped
4 cm (1½ inch) piece ginger, peeled and finely chopped or grated
Juice of 1 lemon
2 Tbsp vegetable oil

Green curry paste
3 green chillies, halved and seeded
4 garlic cloves, roughly chopped
2 handfuls baby spinach leaves
4 cm (1½ inch) piece ginger, peeled and roughly chopped
Juice of 1 lemon
1 bunch coriander (cilantro), roughly chopped
1 bunch mint, roughly chopped
1 tsp ground cumin
1 tsp ground coriander
½ tsp salt, or to taste

Spiced cashews
1 tsp ground turmeric
2 tsp brown sugar
1 Tbsp olive oil
1 tsp cumin seeds
1 tsp salt
1 cup (155 g) cashews

Place the drumsticks in a non-reactive container with the marinade ingredients. Season with a little sea salt and toss with your hands to coat. Cover and refrigerate to marinate for a few hours, or overnight.

For the curry paste, combine all the ingredients in a food processor or blender, season with freshly ground black pepper and blitz till you have a rough paste.

Preheat the oven to 180°C (350°F).

Heat a little oil in a large ovenproof frying pan over high heat (cast iron is perfect for these kinds of dishes) and brown the marinated chicken for a few minutes on each side. Set aside.

Reduce the heat, add a little more oil if needed and add ⅔ cup (225 g) curry paste. Cook, stirring as you go, for a minute or so to release the delicious fragrances. Pour in the coconut milk and stir to combine. Check the flavour and add a little more salt or lemon juice if necessary.

Return the drumsticks to the pan, cover with a lid and place the pan in the oven. Bake for 45 minutes or until the chicken is cooked through. The sauce will have thickened up into the most delicious green curry.

Meanwhile, for the cashews, combine all the ingredients, except the cashews, with 2 tablespoons water in a small jug. Spread the cashews on a baking tray lined with baking paper and pour on the turmeric mixture. Toss everything around to coat well, then place in the oven for the last 20 minutes of cooking. Serve the cashews on the side to be added to the chicken.

Travel advice
How you serve depends on where you serve. If you're on a picnic or at a potluck event, take it straight from the oven and cover tightly with foil, then a couple of tea towels. If your cooler is big enough, put some heat packs (or even a hot water bottle) on the bottom, line with newspaper, then pop your wrapped pan on top. I'd take some flatbreads, warm in a foil pocket, and use these to dip into the sauce and wrap up the chicken to easily eat one-handed. If you're at a sit-down dinner, some cooked rice as a bed would be nice. Either way, you want to enjoy the chicken as a super tasty drumstick and mop up the sauce with roti or rice or similar.

What Can I Bring?

Gently spiced tomato and chickpea soup

I had never loved tomato soup until this one. It comes to us via Paulette Ferrier, a country cook from just over the Queensland border. She made this soup as a starter at an event we were both at and I almost jumped on her for the recipe. Everyone did. The gentle spices, the crunchy sprinkle on top and the filling chickpeas all combine to make this a great meal.

Prep time 15 mins
Cook time 1 hour
Serves 6–8

2 Tbsp olive oil
1 red onion, finely chopped
1 Tbsp finely grated fresh ginger
1 Tbsp finely chopped fresh
  turmeric or 1 tsp ground
  turmeric
4 Tbsp tomato paste
  (concentrated purée)
3 tsp curry powder
2 tsp dried sweet basil
1 tsp sweet paprika
5 cups (1.25 litres) tomato
  passata (puréed tomatoes;
  see Note)
1–2 cups (250–500 ml) good-
  quality chicken or vegetable
  stock
2 × 270 ml (9½ fl oz) tins coconut
  cream
2 × 400 g (14 oz) tins chickpeas,
  drained and rinsed

Nut and seed sprinkle
Olive oil, for cooking
2 handfuls chopped cashews,
  toasted
½ handful sunflower seeds
½ handful sesame seeds
1 tsp curry powder

Start by making the nut and seed sprinkle. Add a good glug of olive oil to a frying pan over medium heat and add the nuts, seeds and curry powder. Toss around with a wooden spoon until toasted to your liking. Season with salt and pepper to taste, then set aside.

Heat the 2 tablespoons of olive oil in a saucepan over medium heat. Add the red onion, ginger and turmeric and cook until the onion is nice and soft, about 10 minutes. Add the tomato paste, curry powder, dried basil and paprika and cook for a few minutes, gently stirring.

Pour in the passata and stock and let it simmer over low heat for at least 40 minutes – the longer the better. Before serving, add the coconut cream and chickpeas and heat through. Scatter with the nut and seed sprinkle.

Travel advice
Pour the soup into a pre-warmed thermos, or thermoses, and transfer warm. Take the nut and seed sprinkle in a small container and scatter on top of the soup to serve.

Note
During summer, when tomatoes are cheap (and if you think of it!), roast up a few trays of halved tomatoes and a few onions, drizzled with olive oil and sprinkled with salt and pepper. Then purée this and freeze to use in the depths of winter in this delicious soup. Otherwise, use the best, most natural passata you can get your hands on. It's such a star element of this recipe that a good one really makes a difference.

The easiest cake in the world

I found this in my late grandmother Helen's recipe box, written out in her beautiful cursive. And with that heading, of course I had to try it. She was right. It is easy - almost entirely made in one saucepan and with just one wooden spoon. But it's also wonderfully delicious (especially with a sharp cheddar and sliced apples - trust me) and lasts for ages. I've made a few adjustments over the years, adding the nuts and soaking the fruit in brandy, which makes it feel a bit more decadent, but you could leave these steps out and it would still be great.

Prep time 10 mins, plus soaking
   and cooling
Cook time 1 hour 15 mins
Serves 8

½ cup (125 ml) brandy
1½ cups (280 g) mixed dried fruit
   (see Note)
½ cup (125 g) butter, cubed
¾ cup (165 g) brown sugar
2 Tbsp treacle, or honey
1 tsp mixed spice
1 tsp ground ginger
1 tsp ground cinnamon
1 tsp bicarbonate of soda
   (baking soda)
2 eggs, lightly beaten
½ cup (75 g) hazelnuts
½ cup (70 g) walnuts, ideally
   dry-toasted in the oven and
   roughly chopped
¾ cup (165 g) uncrystallised
   ginger, finely chopped
1 cup (150 g) plain (all-purpose)
   flour
1 cup (150 g) self-raising flour

Warm the brandy in a saucepan until just simmering. Remove from the heat and add the dried fruit. Leave to plump up for at least 30 minutes.

To your soaked dried fruit, add the butter, sugar, treacle, spices, bicarbonate of soda and ½ cup (125 ml) water. Bring to the boil over medium-high heat, stirring as you go. Set aside to cool for 10 minutes.

Grease and line a 22-24 cm (8½-9½ inch) cake tin with baking paper. Preheat the oven to 180°C (350°F).

Add the eggs and mix to combine. Fold in the hazelnuts, walnuts, ginger and flours, and a pinch of salt. Pour into the cake tin and bake for 1 hour, or until a skewer inserted in the centre comes out clean.

Remove from the oven and cool for 10 minutes before gently removing from the tin.

Travel advice
Once cooled and wrapped tightly in foil, there's not much you can do to spoil this cake. It travels beautifully and lasts for days.

Note
Gran didn't specify which fruit to use, but I like a mixture of dried chopped apricots, figs and cranberries, plus some uncrystallised ginger. Just sultanas would also be great.

A potluck dinner

I love seeing what everyone brings to a potluck dinner, because isn't this kind of generosity and fun what shared tables are all about? Please don't ever feel weird about asking your guests to bring a plate. Everyone loves to contribute and it makes entertaining easy, affordable and collaborative.

One of the loveliest evenings I've had the pleasure of participating in was a potluck dinner at the home of John Monty and Jude Reggett in Rockley, in central western New South Wales. John and Jude live in the nineteenth-century presbytery of St Patrick's Church, and over the years have transformed it into such a special space. The kitchen, with its huge windows and scrubbed wooden table, is my idea of heaven.

Jude and John are wonderful hosts. On this particular night, their beautiful kitchen was full of amazing smells and the glowing candles that they make using their own beeswax, and everywhere neighbours and friends were arriving with food to share.

We started with mugs of soup, and hummus with crusty bread by the fire, then went in to sit around the long table for a candlelit supper, a very memorable group effort!

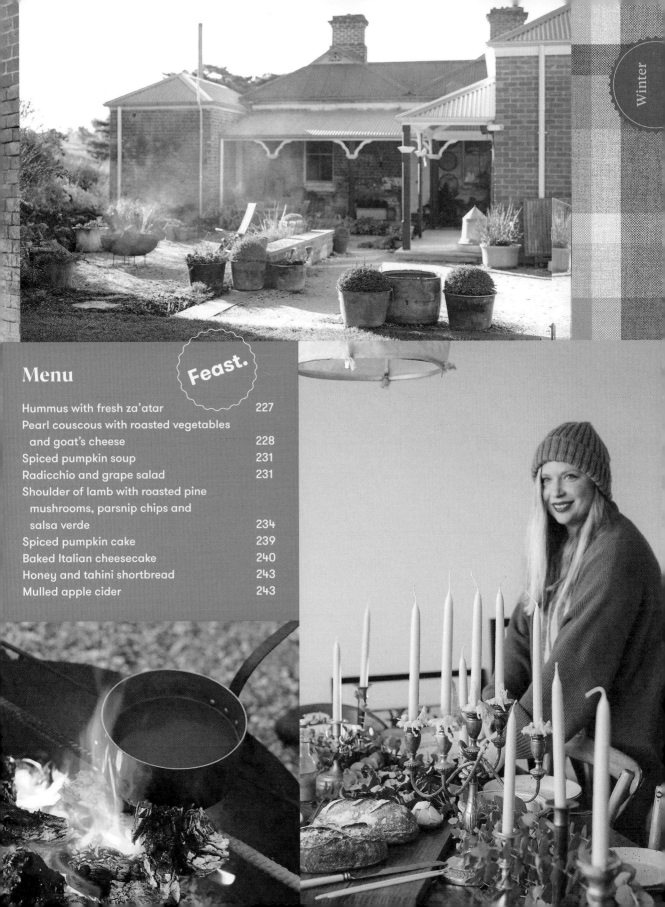

Menu

Feast.

Hummus with fresh za'atar

We've all eaten so much average hummus that when you come across a fluffy, tangy, tasty one like this from Julia Boag, drizzled with fruity olive oil and sprinkled with spices and nuts - well, it's a delicious surprise.

Prep time 20 mins, plus overnight soaking
Cook time 1½–2 hours
Serves 6–8 as a starter

1½ cups (295 g) dried chickpeas, soaked overnight
⅓ cup (80 ml) olive oil
1 garlic clove, chopped
1 Tbsp unhulled tahini
Juice of 1 large lemon
1 tsp ground cumin
1 tsp salt
1 tsp ground black pepper
¼ cup (60 ml) chilled water
Za'atar (see right), to serve

Garnish
A pinch of salt
Drizzle of olive oil
Toasted pine nuts

Drain and rinse the soaked chickpeas, then tip them into a large pot, cover with water and bring to the boil. Reduce the heat and simmer for 1½–2 hours, or until the chickpeas are tender. (The cooking time depends on the freshness of your chickpeas.) Rinse and drain.

Tip into a food processor with the oil, garlic, tahini and lemon juice and blitz until combined. Then add the cumin, salt and pepper and blitz again. While the mixture is blending, add the chilled water in a steady stream until creamy and smooth. Check the flavour and adjust with lemon juice or olive oil until you're happy. Served sprinkled with za'atar, salt, olive oil and pine nuts.

Travel advice
The main thing with hummus is not to serve it 'fridge cold'. Keep it covered at room temperature then spread it on your platter and dress with salt, oil, za'atar and pine nuts right before serving.

Za'atar

Home-made za'atar is a flavour game-changer; everything is amplified and you control how salty or herby you want it. Sprinkle it over hummus (see left), a grain salad, sliced avocado on toast, or anywhere you want some crunch and spice.

Prep time 10 mins
Cook time 5 mins
Makes 1 cup (140 g)

2 Tbsp sesame seeds
1 Tbsp cumin seeds
1 Tbsp coriander seeds
1 Tbsp ground sumac
1 tsp sea salt
2 Tbsp dried oregano
1 tbsp dried thyme

Combine the sesame, cumin and coriander seeds in a dry frying pan and toast over medium heat for a few minutes or until aromatic. Transfer to a mortar and pestle or spice grinder and bash or blitz to a rough crumb. Add the remaining ingredients, stir to combine, then allow to cool and store in an airtight container for up to a month.

Travel advice
Carry it in an airtight container for sprinkling on just about anything.

Pearl couscous with roasted vegetables and goat's cheese

They always say the best parties happen in the kitchen, so don't worry if you need to assemble a dish on-site. Having a job on arrival is also a great way to get warmed up for a night of socialising. The lovely Helen Cosgrove arrived at our potluck dinner with all the ingredients for her fabulous recipe in a cooler bag. Within minutes, she was in the kitchen, glass of wine in hand (thanks, Jude), chatting away while stirring roasted vegetables into cooked pearl couscous, dressing, tasting and plating up her delicious contribution.

Prep time 25 mins
Cook time 55 mins
Serves 6 as a side

1 Tbsp brown sugar
1 Tbsp balsamic vinegar
⅓ cup (80 ml) olive oil
500 g (1 lb 2 oz) cherry
  tomatoes, halved
2 red onions, cut into eighths
1 red capsicum (pepper), cut
  into strips
2 zucchini (courgettes), chopped
  into 2–3 cm (¾–1¼ inch)
  chunks
2 cups (500 ml) chicken or
  vegetable stock, or water
250 g (9 oz) pearl couscous
Juice of 1 lemon
½ cup (60 g) pitted black olives
200 g (7 oz) soft goat's cheese
1 handful roughly chopped flat-
  leaf parsley leaves

Preheat the oven to 140°C (275°F). Mix the brown sugar, balsamic vinegar and 1 tablespoon of the olive oil together in a bowl. Add the tomatoes and toss to coat.

Tip your dressed tomatoes into a roasting tin, season with salt and pepper and pop in the oven for about 35 minutes – you want them to be soft and caramelised but not mushy.

Meanwhile, combine the onion, capsicum and zucchini in another roasting tin. Increase the oven temperature to 180°C (350°F) and season the vegetables with salt and pepper, drizzle with a little more of the olive oil and bake for about 20 minutes or until soft.

While the vegetables are cooking, pour the stock into a saucepan and bring to the boil. Add the couscous and give it a quick stir. Reduce to a simmer, cover with a lid and cook for 10 minutes, or until tender, checking regularly to ensure the couscous doesn't stick to the bottom of the pan or clump together.

Tip the tomatoes into the tin with the vegetables and gently stir together. Drain the couscous and tip into the vegetables. Add a good squeeze of lemon, the rest of the olive oil and the olives, and give it all a final stir. If serving in another dish, transfer to that now then finish with the goat's cheese crumbled over the top and a good sprinkle of parsley.

Travel advice
This dish can be made well in advance, but keep the cheese and parsley to add right at the end. Or you can, as Helen did, pre-roast the vegetables then cook the couscous and assemble on arrival. Whatever's easiest.

Spiced pumpkin soup

There's pumpkin soup, and then there's this pumpkin soup. I am so grateful to Bathurst-based Shylo Land for this recipe, because, as she says, 'it's like a big hug in a bowl'. The coconut milk and paprika give it such a gorgeous mellow flavour.

Prep time 20 mins
Cook time 40 mins
Serves 6–8

2 kg (4 lb 8 oz) pumpkin (squash), peeled and cut into big cubes
2 sweet potatoes, peeled and chopped
1–2 Tbsp olive oil, plus extra for drizzling
4 cups (1 litre) vegetable stock
1 tsp sweet paprika
A pinch of chilli flakes
400 ml (14 fl oz) tin coconut cream
3 Tbsp pepitas (pumpkin seeds)

Preheat the oven to 200°C (400°F).

Put the pumpkin and sweet potato in a roasting tin. Drizzle with the olive oil and roast for 25–30 minutes, or until the vegetables are soft.

Transfer the veggies to a large pot with the stock, paprika, chilli and some salt and pepper. Bring to the boil, uncovered, then reduce the heat and simmer for about 10 minutes.

Blitz the ingredients in a food processor until smooth, then add the coconut cream and adjust the seasoning if needed. Drizzle with a little extra olive oil and sprinkle with pepitas just before serving.

Travel advice
Your host will be stoked if you bring this already hot, in a thermos or insulated dish, ready to pour; hotplate space might be at a premium if this is a big gathering! Even better, bring some small mugs or bowls to share it in.

Radicchio and grape salad

This bitter, sweet and crunchy salad is perfect with the lamb dish on page 234. Thank you to Amanda O'Brien for sharing it with us. Amanda is one of the best bakers, cooks, crafters and hosts I know. She says the idea came from friend, chef Matt Bowrey.

Prep time 10 mins
Cook time NIL
Serves 6–8

2 small radicchio heads
A small bunch of red seedless grapes, halved
1 cup (115 g) walnuts, toasted and roughly chopped
½ cup (80 g) freshly shaved parmesan
⅓ cup (80 ml) extra virgin olive oil
2 Tbsp white wine vinegar

Tear the radicchio leaves in half or thirds and place them on a large platter. Scatter the grapes, walnuts and shaved parmesan over the radicchio leaves.

Combine the oil and vinegar in a small jar and shake well, then dress the salad immediately before serving.

Travel advice
Place the radicchio and grapes in a container and keep the other elements separate to combine and toss on arrival.

*Shoulder of lamb
(page 234)*

Shoulder of lamb with roasted pine mushrooms, parsnip chips and salsa verde

John Monty and Jude Reggett, our hosts for this wintry potluck, really brought the main course energy with this show-stopping lamb dish. These two are such a fantastic entertaining team; Jude has a gift for setting the scene and making everyone feel instantly welcome, and John is the cook, and a very good one at that. Here is his go-to recipe to feed a crowd, something they seem to do often in this village. It is, as he says, 'an easy dish with a generous feel. I love to have it slow-cooking while guests arrive, leaving time to talk and get the party started.'

Prep time 25 mins
Cook time 3 hours 10 mins
Serves 8–10

2 kg (4 lb 8 oz) lamb shoulder
¼ cup (60 ml) olive oil
1 kg (2 lb 4 oz) potatoes, thinly sliced (we don't bother peeling)
2 onions, thinly sliced
4 anchovy fillets
30 g (1 oz) butter, cubed
2–3 garlic heads
1 fresh rosemary sprig, broken into pieces
1½ Tbsp champagne vinegar
Roasted pine mushrooms, Parsnip chips and Salsa verde (see opposite), to serve

Preheat the oven to 180°C (350°F). Rub the lamb with salt and pepper and heat half the oil in a heavy baking dish over moderate–high heat. Brown the lamb all over, then lift it out and set aside.

Layer the potato and onion slices in the bottom of the baking dish and top with the anchovy fillets, remaining oil and butter. Season well with salt and pepper.

Remove only the papery outside of the garlic and cut the heads in half crossways. Push the garlic among the potatoes and onions. Lay the lamb on top, sprinkle with rosemary and vinegar, and pour in 2 cups (500 ml) water.

Cover tightly with foil and bake for 3 hours. Halfway through the cooking time, remove the foil and reduce the heat to 160°C (315°F).

Transfer the lamb to a hot platter with the vegetables. Cut the meat off in chunky pieces and give each person some of the garlic from which they can scoop out the tender flesh to season the lamb.

Serve with roasted pine mushrooms, parsnip chips and salsa verde.

Travel advice

Cook this so it's ready right before departure and keep it in the baking dish, wrapped tightly in foil, then wrapped again with a towel and placed in a basket on top of a heat pack or two. It should stay warm for a while, or reheat on arrival if you can.

• *Pictured page 233*

Roasted pine mushrooms

Pine mushrooms, with their gorgeous saffron-pink colour and delicate flavour, are such a treat served with lamb, but if you can't get your hands on them, brown mushrooms will be fine, too. John's recipe here is excellent in this lamb menu, but would also be delicious served on buttered toast or over pasta.

Prep time 10 mins
Cook time 20 mins
Serves 8 as a side

10 pine or brown mushrooms, sliced into chunks
2 garlic cloves, finely chopped
2 thyme sprigs
1 rosemary sprig
100 g (3½ oz) butter, cubed

Place the mushrooms in a roasting tin and sprinkle with the garlic, thyme, rosemary and butter.

Roast at 180°C (350°F) for 20 minutes, or until all the moisture has evaporated, then serve.

If making these in advance, you can reheat them in the oven at 180°C (350°F) for 5 minutes or until they're starting to go crispy. They can even be frozen ahead of time, then thawed and finished in the oven.

Travel advice
Transport hot if you can (see the advice for lamb, opposite), or slide into the oven on arrival.

Parsnip chips
1. Wash and slice 3 large parsnips into chips.
2. Parboil in a pot of salted water until just tender, then drain and tip into a roasting tin.
3. Drizzle with olive oil and roast at 200°C (400°F) until golden and crisp.

Travel advice
Transport hot from the oven in a thick-walled or insulated container sitting on top of a heat pack.

Salsa verde

Something as rich as delicious slow-roasted lamb really wants a bright, tangy sauce full of acidity and freshness. Enter, John's salsa verde. It's wonderful on so many things, from eggs on toast to potato salads and roasted vegetables to name a few. A jar of this would also be a lovely gift for your host the next time she or he insists that you 'don't bring a thing' but you'd still like to.

Prep time 10 mins
Cook time NIL
Makes approx. 2 cups (500 g)

2 tsp capers, finely chopped
1 garlic clove, finely chopped
4 anchovies, finely chopped
Finely grated zest of 1 lemon
¼ cup (60 ml) champagne vinegar
1 tsp dijon mustard
2 large handfuls basil leaves, very finely chopped
2 large handfuls flat-leaf parsley leaves, very finely chopped
1 large handful mint leaves, very finely chopped
100 ml (3½ fl oz) extra virgin olive oil

Place the capers, garlic, anchovies and lemon zest in a bowl. Add the vinegar and mustard and stir to combine, then add the herbs and pour in the oil. Stir, then season to taste.

Travel advice
Store in a clean jar and keep chilled until needed.

Tips for organising your own potluck

1. Perhaps suggest a style of cooking, a country or a cookbook for your guests to take inspiration from.

2. Delegate the stages of your meal: put someone on starters, mains, sides, salads and dessert. And if any friends are less enthused about covering a course, put them on bread, ice, ice cream – that kind of thing.

3. And from Jude: 'When hosting a potluck dinner, it's helpful to have a theme but don't be too rigid about it. Allocate people a course and then appreciate everything that arrives. Light lots of candles, play music and enjoy sharing your home, garden and space with your friends.'

Spiced pumpkin cake

'In the country, people always want to share with you,' says Georgie, another of Jude and John's creative, clever friends. 'It might be produce from the garden, garden clippings or a loved book. This cake is my way of saying thank you, welcome, happy birthday - anything. Last autumn, I was in a pickle because one of the legs on the dining table at my B & B had collapsed, and I had people checking in that afternoon. My friend Gerard drove straight over and fixed it. When I asked him what the bill was he replied, a cake. So this is what I made!'

Prep time 20 mins
Cook time 1 hour 15 mins
Serves 8–10

450 g (1 lb) pumpkin (squash),
  peeled and diced
1⅔ cups (250 g) plain
  (all-purpose) flour
2 tsp baking powder
1 tsp bicarbonate of soda
  (baking soda)
A pinch of salt
2 tsp ground ginger
2 tsp ground cinnamon
½ tsp ground nutmeg
¼ tsp ground cardamom
225 ml (7¾ fl oz) good-quality
  olive oil, plus extra for greasing
4 large eggs
200 g (7 oz) brown sugar
1½ tsp vanilla extract

Icing
250 g (9 oz) full-fat cream
  cheese, softened to room
  temperature
115 g (4 oz) butter, softened to
  room temperature
300 g (10½ oz) icing
  (confectioners') sugar
1 tsp vanilla extract
1 tsp sea salt flakes
½ cup (60 g) walnuts

Steam the pumpkin pieces until soft then mash as finely as you can.

Preheat the oven to 180°C (350°F). Grease and line a 23 cm (9 inch) round cake tin with baking paper.

Whisk the flour, baking powder, bicarbonate of soda, salt and spices together in a large bowl, then set aside. Whisk the olive oil, eggs, brown sugar, steamed pumpkin and vanilla together until combined. Pour the wet ingredients into the dry ingredients and use an electric mixer or whisk to beat until completely combined.

Spread the batter into the tin and bake for 50–60 minutes, or until a skewer inserted in the middle of the cake comes out clean. If you find the top or edges of the cake are browning too quickly in the oven, loosely cover with foil. Remove the cake from the oven and allow it to cool completely.

To make the icing, use an electric mixer or stand mixer to beat the cream cheese and butter together on high speed until smooth and creamy. Add the sugar, vanilla and salt. Beat on low speed for 30 seconds, then switch to high speed and beat for a couple of minutes. Spread the icing on the cooled cake and decorate with the walnuts.

Travel advice
This cake, even iced, is made of sturdy stuff so should travel pretty well. However, if it's a warm day, keep it chilled so the cream cheese icing doesn't melt.

Baked Italian cheesecake

Rhonda Gillen is a wonderful, creative and generous cook, and I'm grateful to her for sharing this cheesecake recipe in particular because it is so, so delicious. I now take my cue from her and bake, take and share this cheesecake in a ceramic dish (her husband, Brian, a potter, made the blue and white bowl here). It just makes transporting it so much easier - and more stable!

Prep time 20 mins, plus soaking, resting and chilling
Cook time 1 hour 20 mins
Serves 8

50 g (1¾ oz) sultanas
70 ml (2¼ fl oz) sherry or port
250 g (9 oz) mascarpone cheese
1 kg (2 lb 4 oz) ricotta cheese
⅔ cup (150 g) caster (superfine) sugar
3 large eggs
1 tsp vanilla paste
2 Tbsp plain (all-purpose) flour

Pastry
2⅓ cups (350 g) plain (all-purpose) flour, plus extra for dusting
100 g (3½ oz) icing (confectioners') sugar
175 g (6 oz) unsalted butter, cubed
1 egg, beaten

Place the sultanas and sherry in a bowl for 1 hour. Drain, reserving 1 tablespoon of the sherry.

For the pastry, combine the flour and icing sugar in the bowl of a food processor, or in a large bowl. Add the butter and mix until it resembles breadcrumbs. Add the beaten egg and blitz until the mixture comes together into a dough. Shape into a ball, wrap and refrigerate for 1–2 hours.

Lightly dust your work surface and roll out the dough big enough to fit a 22–24 cm (8½–9½ inch) flan or cake tin with 4 cm (1½ inches) of overhang. Place in the fridge to chill for a further 30 minutes.

Preheat the oven to 180°C (350°F).

Line the pastry shell with baking paper and fill with pastry weights, or uncooked rice or pulses. Blind bake for 10 minutes, then remove the weights and bake for another 10 minutes or until the pastry feels dry. Reduce the oven temperature to 160°C (315°F).

Mix the mascarpone, ricotta and caster sugar together in a bowl until smooth. Add the eggs, one at a time, stirring well between each addition. Fold in the vanilla, flour, sultanas and reserved sherry until the mixture is smooth and thick.

Pour this mixture into the pastry case and bake for 1 hour, or until the top feels 'set' and is a lovely golden brown.

Turn the oven off and leave the cheesecake inside to cool for 1 hour. Stick a wooden spoon in the oven door to hold it slightly ajar. Transfer the cheesecake to the fridge to cool completely – for at least 3 hours – before slicing.

Travel advice
Take this in the dish you baked it in, just wrap tightly in plastic wrap and bring to room temperature before slicing and sharing around.

Honey and tahini shortbread

Inspired by a recipe from Adam Liaw, Amanda often makes and brings these to parties and I can see why. They have such a great sesame flavour thanks to the tahini, are nice and short due to all that lovely butter, and deliver a mellow sweetness cut with flakes of salt.

Prep time 20 mins
Cook time 15 mins
Makes approx. 20–25

200 g (7 oz) salted butter, at room temperature
80 g (2¾ oz) brown sugar
80 g (2¾ oz) caster (superfine) sugar
125 g (4½ oz) honey
125 g (4½ oz) tahini
330 g (11¾ oz) plain (all-purpose) flour
1 tsp baking powder
½ tsp salt
Sea salt flakes, for sprinkling

Preheat the oven to 170°C (325°F) and line two baking trays with baking paper.

Combine the butter and sugars in the bowl of a stand mixer fitted with the paddle attachment, or use a large bowl and an electric mixer. Beat until light and creamy then add the honey and tahini and beat again, stopping to scrape down the side of the bowl.

Sift in the flour, baking powder and salt, and mix until you have a stiff dough.

Roll the dough into small balls (about 20 g/¾ oz). Place on the baking trays with room between each for spreading. Press each biscuit with the tines of a fork to flatten a little and sprinkle with the sea salt.

Bake for 15 minutes, making sure to turn the trays around halfway through, especially if your oven doesn't cook evenly.

Travel advice
Cool then store in a jar or airtight container lined with paper towel to stop the shortbread softening.

Note
I make the amount of biscuits I need then freeze the remaining dough for future use.

Mulled apple cider

Tania Robinson, another of Jude and John's lovely neighbours, says of this incredibly fragrant cider recipe, 'We make this in autumn and winter from the left-over apples we store from our trees, or from roadside foraging. It's usually a mix of old-fashioned varieties, their sweetness depending on how much late-summer sun they got.' Besides being a great belly- and hand-warmer on a crisp winter evening, this spiced cider will fill your home with the most wonderful, welcoming smell.

Prep time 10 mins
Cook time 45 mins
Serves 8–12

12–14 apples, quartered (no need to peel or core)
⅓ cup (115 g) raw honey, or ⅓ cup (75 g) brown sugar, or to taste
4 cinnamon sticks
12 whole cloves
12 allspice berries
7 whole cardamom pods
1 whole nutmeg
Zest of 1 lemon, peeled with a vegetable peeler to avoid the white pith
Rum or brandy (optional)

Place all the ingredients in a large, heavy-based pot or Dutch oven and fill with just enough water to cover the apples. Simmer for 45 minutes or until the apples can be mashed with a fork. Remove from the heat and mash with a potato masher.

Strain the cider through a fine-mesh sieve or piece of muslin over a large bowl. You can squeeze out the juice, but don't squeeze out too much pulp or the cider will be too thick. Discard the pulp and spices.

Reheat in a pot (preferably over a campfire) to serve hot. Add a splash of rum or brandy (for the grown-ups) just before serving. Store any remaining cider in glass bottles (we re-use our old passata/puréed tomato bottles) in the fridge for up to 1 week.

Travel advice
Heat at home then pack in a thermos to keep warm or bring your own little saucepan to heat on arrival.

Recipe contributors

Laura Corcoran, Boorowa NSW
Cook and caterer
@los_kitchen
Classic sausage rolls, page 28;
Tuna bites, page 31; Vanilla
butterfly cakes, page 32

Annette Dinicola, Griffith NSW
Almond orchardist and cook
@mandoleorchard
Gluten-free almond milk
cheesecake, page 42

Elise Cook, Sydney NSW
Cook and bakery owner
@thebakeryonglenayr
Honey seed slice, page 48

Erin Davis, Marburg QLD
*Founder, The Great Marburg
Bake Off*
@thegreatmarburgbakeoff
The Great Marburg Bake Off
chocolate cake, page 51

Michelle Lim, Boorowa NSW
Cook and organic garlic producer
@misha_rose_bites
Pork belly sisig, page 58; Lamb
kaldereta, page 61; Pandan
chicken, page 62; Leche flan,
page 65; Pavlova, page 65;
Buko pandan, page 66; Crinkle
biscuits, page 69

**Kristine Lindbjerg Hansen,
Capertee NSW**
Graphic designer and artist
@lindbjerggraphic
Rhubarb and marzipan crumble,
page 85

**Vladka Bartyzal,
Wollongong NSW**
Baker
@vladkabartyzal
Czech yeasted plum cake, page 86

**Jean-François Esnault,
Mudgee NSW**
Winemaker
@oliveatwist and
@skimstonewines
Really, really good roast chicken
with orange and bay, page 102;
Ratatouille, page 105; Sugar
crêpes, page 106

Ed Swift, Orange NSW
Winery co-owner
@printhiewines
Elderflower gin cocktail,
page 112

**Nanae Harada and Robbie
Robinson, Orange NSW**
*Foragers and cooks specialising
in Japanese fine foods*
@mountainmiso_nanaeharada
Miso mushroom bruschetta,
page 137

**Angela and Ehren Lyons,
Tumbarumba NSW**
*Flower farm gardeners and
B & B operators*
@thelaurelhillfarm
Jam roll, raspberry and dark
chocolate cake, page 151

**Laura Fraumeni,
Tumbarumba NSW**
*Cafe, boutique cinema and
bookshop owner*
@nestcinemacafe
Spiced hot chocolate, page 151

Amanda Thomas, Warren NSW
Farmer
Slow-cooked lamb shanks, page 164;
Fried mixed potatoes, page 167

Rachel Saliba, Gulgong NSW
*Horticulturalist and organic
garlic farmer*
@gulgonggarlic
Toum, page 170; Labne with
crunchy vegetables, page 170;
Fattoush, page 175

Reanne O'Rourke, Gulgong NSW
Ceramic artist
@thisfarmhouseceramics
Lamb koftas, page 171; Sambousek,
page 172

Ree Booth, Mozart NSW
Mother/chauffeur to my kids, farmer and Airbnb host/manager
@thehareandhoundau
Braised beef short ribs, page 194; Roasted pumpkin with dukkah, page 198; Brussels sprouts with bacon, page 198; Boiled eggs with bacon, page 198; Almond and lime syrup cake, page 202; Irish coffee mix, page 205

Sophie Comiskey, Rockley NSW
Farmer, producer, mum, wife and maker of nourishing food
@sophie_comiskey
Orange and honey glazed ham, page 197; Garlic bread, page 198; Roasted garlic potatoes, page 198; Meringue-topped chocolate cake, page 206

Clare Lee, Quirindi NSW
Agritourism manager and granola cook
@windystationwoolshed and @fare_on_the_plains
Beef tagine with coconut quinoa, page 217

Paulette Ferrier, Stanthorpe QLD
Orchardist and cook
Gently spiced tomato and chickpea soup, page 221

Julia Boag, Millthorpe NSW
Antique-store owner
@thebowermillthorpe
Hummus with fresh za'atar, page 227

Helen Cosgrove, Goulburn NSW
Interior designer
@studio.2580
Pearl couscous with roasted vegetables and goat's cheese, page 228

Shylo Land, Bathurst NSW
Pilates instructor and boutique owner
@shylomarieandco
Spiced pumpkin soup, page 231

Amanda O'Brien, Oberon NSW
B & B co-owner, cook and farmer
@homefarmcabin
Radicchio and grape salad, page 231; Honey and tahini shortbread, page 243

John Monty and Jude Reggett, Rockley NSW
John and Jude run The Feel Good Farm and are big contributors to their community artisan markets and the Rockley Gardens and Art Festival
@montidon and @thefeelgoodfarm
Shoulder of lamb with roasted pine mushrooms, parsnip chips and salsa verde, page 234

Georgina Stuart, Edith NSW
B & B host
@bimlowcottage
Spiced pumpkin cake, page 239

Rhonda Gillen, Edith NSW
Preserver, baker and maker
@rhonda_gillen
Baked Italian cheesecake, page 240

Tania Robinson, Rockley NSW
Designer and scent-seeker
@southernwildco
Mulled apple cider, page 243

Acknowledgements

I'd like to firstly acknowledge the Wiradjuri people on whose Country I live and wrote this book. I pay my respects to the Wiradjuri Nation, their Elders past and present, and extend that respect to all First Nations people on whose land we work, live and gather. Thank you.

This book is all about generosity. It's about sharing our spaces, recipes, tables and time. It's about getting together even when we're busy, or when funds are limited, or when we're disinclined to cook for a crowd or a few. It's about the generosity of friends who bring good things to our tables and how the whole experience is all the richer for it.

And speaking of bringing good things to the table, thank you to all the country cooks who have generously shared their special recipes in these pages. I am so grateful to you all. From Michelle Lim's Pork belly sisig to Ree Booth's Almond and lime syrup cake; Jean-François's insanely good roast chook to Clare Lee's tagine, to name but a few. All are such personal and special recipes – all with their own stories and evolutions – and all now favourites of mine, too. These are recipes I will cook and share again and again. I hope you will, too.

Still on generosity, thank you to the incredible team at Murdoch Books. This is my fourth book with you, and I still pinch myself at the opportunity to collaborate with such talented and kind professionals. Jane, Justine, Andrea, Kristy and Sharon, I have loved making this book with you.

And, finally, a big thank you to Tim, Alice and Tommy: my family, and my favourite people to cook for. I love you so much, and kids, as you insist on growing into adults and away from home, please know that I'll always want to bring food to your tables, wherever you are.

Index

What Can I Bring?

Published in 2024 by Murdoch Books,
an imprint of Allen & Unwin

Murdoch Books Australia
Cammeraygal Country
83 Alexander Street
Crows Nest NSW 2065
Phone: +61 (0)2 8425 0100
murdochbooks.com.au
info@murdochbooks.com.au

Murdoch Books UK
Ormond House
26–27 Boswell Street
London WC1N 3JZ
Phone: +44 (0) 20 8785 5995
murdochbooks.co.uk
info@murdochbooks.co.uk

For corporate orders and custom publishing,
contact our business development team at
salesenquiries@murdochbooks.com.au

Publisher: Jane Morrow
Editorial manager: Justine Harding
Design manager: Kristy Allen
Designer: Sharon Misko
Editor: Andrea O'Connor
Photography: Sophie Hansen
Additional photography: Pip Farquharson
@photographybypip, front cover, pages 7,
90–3, 96–7, 139 (image of Sophie), 144–5, 176;
Georgina Gavel @creativebygeorge, page 220
(image of Sophie)
Fabric designers (front cover and internals):
Cecilia Mok, Schatzi Brown
Production director: Lou Playfair

Murdoch Books acknowledges the Traditional Owners
of the Country on which we live and work. We pay our
respects to all Aboriginal and Torres Strait Islander
Elders, past and present.

ISBN 978 1 92261 639 5

 A catalogue record for this
book is available from the
National Library of Australia

Colour reproduction by Splitting Image Colour Studio
Pty Ltd, Wantirna, Victoria
Printed by 1010 Printing International Limited, China

OVEN GUIDE: You may find cooking times vary
depending on the oven you are using. For fan-forced
ovens, as a general rule, set the oven temperature to
20°C (35°F) lower than indicated in the recipe.

IMPORTANT: Those who might be at risk from the
effects of salmonella poisoning (the elderly, pregnant
women, young children and those suffering from immune
deficiency diseases) should consult their doctor with any
concerns about eating raw eggs. Please ensure that all
seafood and beef to be eaten raw or lightly cooked are
very fresh and of the highest quality.

TABLESPOON MEASURES: We have used 20 ml
(4 teaspoon) tablespoon measures. If you are using a
15 ml (3 teaspoon) tablespoon add an extra teaspoon
of the ingredient for each tablespoon specified.

10 9 8 7 6 5 4 3

MIX
Paper | Supporting
responsible forestry
FSC® C016973

'The best kind of bring-a-plate gathering is around a big table, everyone all squished in, passing the food around, super relaxed, lots of chatter, laughs and hopefully some left-over dessert for breakfast the next day!'

Angela and Ehren Lyons
Jam roll, raspberry and dark chocolate cake, page 151

'WHEN PEOPLE SAY "DON'T BRING ANYTHING", I BRING A BOTTLE OF LOCAL WINE AND SOMETHING SEASONAL FROM THE GARDEN, VEGGIE PATCH OR KITCHEN – USUALLY EGGS, JAM, SOURDOUGH, BOTTLED FRUIT, A BOUQUET GARNI, VEGGIES OR FLOWERS.'

Amanda O'Brien
Radicchio and grape salad, page 231

made with love

'WHEN PEOPLE SAY "DON'T BRING ANYTHING", I BRING A HOME-MADE LEMON CHEESECAKE WITH FRESH STRAWBERRIES AND CREAM. IT'S ALWAYS WELL RECEIVED, AND CRUMBS ARE THE ONLY BIT LEFT OVER.'

Reanne O'Rourke
Lamb koftas, page 171

'The best kind of bring-a-plate gathering is held outdoors, with a focus on meaningful conversations. We would never have a gathering that didn't finish with a G&T.'

Kristine Lindbjerg Hansen
Rhubarb and marzipan crumble, page 85

'I use baskets with wooden chopping boards underneath hot dishes and an esky lined with freezer bricks for cold dishes.'

Ree Booth
Braised beef short ribs, page 194

GATHER YOUR FRIENDS & FAMILY